The Vastness of
Natural Languages

The Vastness of Natural Languages

D. TERENCE LANGENDOEN
and
PAUL M. POSTAL

Basil Blackwell

© D. Terence Langendoen and Paul M. Postal 1984

First published 1984
Basil Blackwell Publisher Limited
108 Cowley Road, Oxford OX4 1JF, England

British Library Cataloguing in Publication Data

Langendoen, D. Terence
 The vastness of natural languages.
 1. Mathematical linguistics
 I. Title   II. Postal, Paul M.
 410   P138

  ISBN 0-631-13461-1

Typeset by Santype International Ltd., Salisbury, Wilts.
Printed in Great Britain by
The Camelot Press Ltd, Southampton

Contents

Preface

This monograph argues that the collection of sentences comprising each individual natural language (NL) is so vast that its magnitude is not given by any number, finite or transfinite. This means that NLs cannot, as is currently almost universally assumed, be considered recursively enumerable, hence countable (denumerable) collections of sentences. For if they were such, the magnitude of each would be no greater than the smallest transfinite cardinal number $\aleph_0$. It then follows that there can be no procedure, algorithm, Turing machine or grammar that constructs or generates all the members of an NL, since, by definition, such a procedure, algorithm, Turing machine or grammar can construct or generate only recursively enumerable, hence countable, collections. A system which constructs some NL sentences must inevitably leave most NL sentences unconstructed.

Linguistic research over the past quarter century has been largely guided by two major assumptions introduced by N. Chomsky: (i) that the best theory of NLs is a theory of grammars that generates NLs and (ii) that human beings know an NL in virtue of knowing a grammar that generates it. These assumptions cannot be maintained. The only adequate theories of NLs are, we contend, those that posit non-constructive or non-generative grammars. The theorems of such theories are truths about NLs in general or about particular NLs; one of these theorems states that no procedure, algorithm, Turing machine or grammar can construct or generate all the sentences of any NL. Accordingly, if human knowledge of NLs were limited to what internalized grammars can generate, then that knowledge would be extraordinarily deficient. Put differently, if psychologically real (internalized) grammars are generative, then those grammars describe not NLs, but at best only proper subcollections of NLs.

If NLs are merely recursively enumerable collections of sentences, then Chomsky's two major assumptions are compelling. A grammar that generates the sentences of a recursively enumerable collection is, first, a complete theory of that collection in the sense that no sentence of the collection is left out. Second, to account for the remarkable ability of human beings to decide the grammatical properties of enormously many NL sentences, they may reasonably be supposed to have the ability to generate representations of those sentences; under ideal conditions, the procedures that underlie that ability could then be used to determine the grammatical properties of any NL sentence whatever. However, the appeal of Chomsky's assumptions should not obscure their dependence on the even more basic assumption that NLs are recursively enumerable (hence denumerable) collections. This assumption is, we maintain, false, and any implications drawn from it, no matter how appealing or widespread, are inevitably also at least partly in error.

This study had its origins in several strands of work: (i) efforts to make precise the notion generative grammar and the collections that such grammars generate (see Langendoen (1976, 1982)), (ii) the discovery that there are essential truths about NLs that are not expressible within any theory of generative grammar; (iii) efforts to develop a non-constructive theory of grammar (see Johnson and Postal (1980); Postal (1982)), and (iv) realization that the truths about NLs that are not expressible constructively are expressible non-constructively. Finally, this work has been influenced and inspired by Katz's work on the abstract character of NLs; see Katz (1977, 1978, 1980, and especially 1981, 1983). Although one does not have to accept platonic realism to accept the conclusions drawn here about the vastness of NLs, the two go very naturally together. Moreover, the only conceivable rational basis for rejecting our conclusions is the adoption of an ontological commitment (nominalism or some version of conceptualism) so narrow that it either does not recognize the existence of certain objects claimed here to be NL sentences, or else, without justification, excludes these objects from the proper realm of linguistics.

Our conclusion concerning the vastness of NLs is based on a demonstration of a strict parallelism between the collection of all sentences of an NL and the collection of all sets. The discovery around the turn of this century that the latter collection is not itself a set led to fundamental reforms in logic and the foundations of mathematics. The same reasoning that establishes that the collection of all sets cannot itself be a set (a collection with fixed magnitude, finite or transfinite) also establishes that the collection of all NL sentences cannot be a set. Consequently, fundamental revisions of currently standard views of NLs and grammars are required for reasons similar to those that operated in the foundations of logic and mathematics. For readers who are unfamiliar with set theory or who wish to refresh their memories, chapter 1 provides a brief outline of the relevant aspects of set theory and a discussion of their relevance to linguistic issues.

Chapter 2 points out that the standard linguistic assumption that NLs are infinite recursively enumerable collections of sentences each of finite length (size) has been defended against the position that NLs are finite collections of sentences each shorter than some fixed finite length. However, practically no arguments have been given against the position that NLs are non-denumerable collections of sentences, some (in fact, most) of which are of transfinite length. Chapter 3 examines the arguments in the literature that purport to show that there can be no *finite* length limitation on NL sentences. Most of these arguments are unsound; however, one argument is not only sound but generalizes to show that there is no *transfinite* length limitation on NL sentences either.

Chapter 4 demonstrates that the classical proof that the collection of all sets itself is not a set also shows that the collection of all sentences of any NL is also not a set. This demonstration reveals a property of NLs that is inexpressible by any constructive or generative theory of NLs. Indeed, each generative theory of NLs entails that NLs do not have the property in question.

Chapter 5 draws out certain consequences for linguistic theory of the argument in chapter 4, taking up such matters as the incorrectness of almost all contemporary theories of NL grammars, the character of non-constructive grammars of NLs, and the effability and learnability of NLs. Chapter 6 considers whether the implications of the main result of this study can be avoided by adopting one or another non-platonist view about the nature of NLs. We contend that none of these ontologies offers any insight into the nature of NLs nor any insight into the relation of NLs to human beings or to human knowledge of NLs that is not available within the framework proposed here. Since each of these alternatives requires arbitrary imposition of a restriction on the size of NL sentences otherwise not required, the conclusions drawn about the vastness of NLs are shown to be unavoidable. Finally, chapter 7 considers the issue of transfinite sentences from a different point of view, arguing that any approach which attempts to place them beyond the bounds of linguistic study yields absurdities. It also takes up the question of the essential unity of the realms of finite and transfinite sentences for each NL.

We would like to offer our special thanks to Jerrold Katz and Arnold Koslow for helpful discussions of the issues involved in this study. We are also grateful to David Johnson, Edward Keenan and Warren Plath for many useful comments on earlier versions of this work. Any remaining errors are ours, not theirs.

1

Set – Theoretical Background

1.1 Collections and their magnitudes

Collections are ensembles of distinct entities or objects of any sort.[1] The elements encompassed by a fixed collection are said to be its members or elements. They belong to the collection. Collections are determined by their members. Two collections are identical if and only if they have the same members. Given any collection, it is possible to question its magnitude, to ask how many elements belong to it. One can think of such determinations of quantity as placing the collection in a one-to-one correspondence[2] with a restricted sequence of numbers. Take the sequence of non-negative integers:

(1)   0, 1, 2, 3, 4, ...

The magnitude of any finite collection is given by the highest positive integer of the minimal initial sequence of (1) required so that there is some one-to-one correspondence between the members of the collection and that initial sequence, with the proviso that no element can be put in correspondence with 0.

---

[1] We explain below why we use the uncommon term 'collection' instead of the expected 'set'. Our usage corresponds to the 'aggregate' of many mathematical writings and to the sense of 'class' found in older logical writings.

[2] One-to-one correspondences are types of binary relations, moreover, types of functions, sometimes called *bijections*. See Lewis and Papadimitriou (1981: 8–11), Halmos (1960: 32).

Consider the collections characterized in (2):

(2) a. Round squares
     b. Cities in France whose populations exceed four
         million in 1980
     c. Things which are one of the letters A, B, C, or D

Round squares can be put in one-to-one correspondence with an initial subsequence of (1) whose only member is 0, since there are no round squares ... the collection in question is empty. A one-to-one correspondence between two collections requires that every member of one correspond to a unique member of the other and conversely. Such a condition is vacuously satisfied by collections without members, since, viewed extensionally, there is only one collection without members. And every collection is obviously in one-to-one correspondence with itself. The collection of French cities in (2b) yields the one-to-one correspondence.[3]

(3)   1
                          Paris

since Paris is the only entity meeting the condition, and thus the collection has a magnitude of 1. The collection in (2c) yields the correspondence in (4) and so has a magnitude of four.

(4)   1, 2, 3, 4
                           A, B, C, D

The notion of one-to-one correspondence has been illustrated for *finite* collections, those whose elements could in principle be *listed*. However, we characterized the collections in (2) by giving *conditions* or *complex predicates*, which define collections via satisfaction. Everything meeting the condition is in the collection; nothing else is. More precisely, such conditions can be regarded as statement schemata ('open sentences'), containing exactly one unbound variable, each of which determines a collection via

---

[3] Of course, (3) is actually a correspondence between the names of the integer 1 and of the French city. But, as these names are in one-to-one correspondence with the objects they name, the correspondence is established.

instantiation of its variable. Thus, (2b) is equivalent to:

(5)   x is a city in France whose population exceeds four
      million in 1980

The collection defined by (5) contains some object Ob if and only
if (5) holds of Ob. More generally, a condition defines a collection
encompassing all and only the elements for which the condition
holds. Since contradictory conditions, such as 'x is not identical to
x', have no true instantiations – hold for no objects – all such
conditions define the null collection.

While conditions like (5) are intensional – give the definitional
requirements for belonging – collections are extensional, involve
the actual elements. Consequently, *distinct* conditions may define
the same collection. So (2b) = (5) and the *intensionally* distinct
characterization in (6) determine the same collection.

(6)   x is a city which is a capital of France in 1980

Some collections can be specified directly, with minimal appeal to
intensional characterizations, that is, can be listed. Instead of (2c),
we might have simply given (7), where the printed ordering of
elements is arbitrary and irrelevant:

(7)   B, A, C, D

Collections characterizable by lists are, informally, *finite* collections.[4]

While we have dealt so far with finite collections, it has been
known (in fact proved),[5] at least since antiquity, that some collections are not finite, that is, cannot be put in one-to-one correspondence with any *terminated* initial subsequence of the sequence in
(1). This is evidently true of the collection of elements forming the
sequence of non-negative integers itself. A simple proof that this
collection is not finite is given by Russell (1903: 357). Assume the

---

[4] Formal definitions of *infinite* sets characterize them as those which can be put
in one-to-one correspondence with one of their *proper* subsets. In these terms,
finite sets are just those which are not infinite.

[5] For example, Euclid proved that there are infinitely many primes. See Hardy
(1941: 32–4) for some discussion.

contrary. Then some finite integer, say N, is last in the sequence, and provides itself the number giving the magnitude of the set of non-negative integers. But the number of integers from 0 to N is N + 1, which is greater than N. So, the hypothesis that N is the largest non-negative integer leads to the contradiction that it is not, and, consequently, is false. Since the sequence of integers from 0 to N cannot be put in one-to-one correspondence with the sequence from 1 to N as required, there is then no finite collection of all the elements in the progression of integers. Russell took this to be a formal proof of the existence of infinite collections. However, his reasoning here was informal and, when made precise, it would be clear, as in formalized set theories, that the conclusion that there is an infinite collection of integers, hence infinite collections in general, only follows via tacit assumptions not explicit in the account just given. Internal to set theories, infinite sets can be shown to exist only via axioms (so called 'axioms of infinity') which postulate their existence more or less directly; see Fraenkel, Bar-Hillel and Levy (1973: 46).

Significantly, the notion of magnitude relevant to infinite collections is, just as for finite collections, characterizable via the notion one-to-one correspondence. For instance, the fact that the collections of positive, even positive and odd positive integers can all be put in one-to-one correspondence shows that these have the same (non-finite) magnitude. Or, less circularly, the existence of some one-to-one correspondence between them is what is meant by saying they have the same (non-finite) magnitude:

(8)   a.   1, 2, 3, 4, 5, 6, ...
             b.   2, 4, 6, 8, 10, 12, ...
             c.   1, 3, 5, 7, 9, 11, ...

In short, the notion of magnitude carries over to non-finite collections. Collections with the magnitude of those in (8) are called *denumerable*, or *countably infinite*.

Until relatively recently, it was generally believed that *any* non-finite collection is countably infinite and thus that there is only a single transfinite magnitude. As Fraenkel (1966: 18–19) puts it: 'Thus the conjecture ... that *all* infinite sets might be equivalent, gains additional weight. If this conjecture, which up to the 1870's had been tacitly assumed to be self-evident ...' But, in the 1870s,

Georg Cantor[6] showed that there was a collection with a greater magnitude than those in (8), that known as the *continuum*, the number of points on a line or, equivalently, the number of real numbers between e.g. 0 and 1. Cantor's proof of the non-denumerability of the continuum showed the existence of at least two transfinite magnitudes.[7] Later he demonstrated that for any collection of any fixed magnitude, it is possible to find a still larger one.

Cantor's proof of the general case can be sketched as follows. Let the collection of all subcollections of an arbitrary collection X be designated C(X). One collection A is a subcollection of another B if and only if every element of A is an element of B. Cantor showed that for any collection Q, C(Q) is of a higher magnitude than Q. The special case that there is a greater magnitude than that of the collection of positive integers immediately follows. The proof of the general result, known as *Cantor's Theorem*, proceeds by showing that (i), C(Q) must have at least as many members as Q, and (ii) C(Q) and Q cannot be put into one-to-one correspondence. The demonstration of (i) is trivial, for C(Q) always contains all those single-element collections whose members are the elements of Q. So, if Q is the collection in (7), C(Q) will include, from the definition of 'C(X)', each of the four singleton collections having as members either A, B, C or D. Note that an element E is not to be confused with the collection whose only member is E. The demonstration of (ii) is relatively straightforward as well. See Eisenberg (1971: 221), Fraenkel (1966: 42–3), Halmos (1960: 93), Lewis and Papadimitriou (1981: 28) and Wall (1972: 182–3).

Apparently then, for any collection W, C(W) is of a greater magnitude. The magnitude of a collection having a fixed magnitude is referred to as its *cardinality*, or *power*, and it may seem natural that each collection be associated with some fixed power. But see below. The collections in (2a, b, c) are associated with the respective finite cardinals 0, 1, 4; those in (8) are associated with the (transfinite) cardinal Cantor called $\aleph_0$. The continuum has a

---

[6] For an introductory discussion, see Fraenkel (1966). Cantor's relevant works are translated and reprinted as Cantor (1952).

[7] The proof is based on Cantor's famous diagonalization argument, now a fundamental mathematico-logical tool. For discussions, see Boolos and Jeffrey (1974: 11–18), Fraenkel (1966: 21–3), Hopcroft and Ullman (1979: 182–3), Kleene (1952: 6–8), and Lewis and Papadimitriou (1981: 27–8).

higher power. In general, for a collection V with power n, the power of C(V) is designated 2^n. For finite collections, this has a clear arithmetical interpretation, as the reader can verify. For discussion and application to non-finite collections, see Boolos and Jeffrey (1974: 11–14), Fraenkel (1966: 21–3), Kleene (1952: 6–8), Lewis and Papadimitriou (1981: 27–8) and Wall (1972: 184–6).

1.2   Sets and paradoxes

We have so far used the non-standard term 'collection', where the reader might have expected the familiar and standard usage 'set'. We now clarify the basis for this distinction. The notion of collection which we have introduced is essentially the traditional idea of *class*, still referred to under this name in some modern works, such as Eisenberg (1971), and equivalent to Cantor's concept of set. The discovery that this notion yielded various 'paradoxes', in fact, contradictions, showed that unrestricted use of it is not possible. One cannot make the uncritical assumption that every condition determines a set, that is, a collection capable of being an element of other collections. Specifically, a traditional idea, which was accepted until the end of the nineteenth century, and which seems a priori natural, is that there is a collection which contains absolutely everything. Similarly, it was assumed that there is a collection which contains (just) all non-null collections. These two collections may be characterized by the respective conditions:

(9)   a.   x is identical to x
           b.   There is a y which is a member of x

Despite the seemingly intuitive character of such collections, a fundamental result of Cantor's work, or, more accurately, of the work it influenced, particularly, Russell's (1903), is that unrestricted appeal to collections like those defined by (9a, b) cannot be accepted. More precisely, taking such collections to be elements of other collections leads to contradiction. One such contradiction, known as Cantor's Paradox, is largely derivable from Cantor's Theorem.[8]

---

[8] A rigorous derivation of Cantor's Paradox is given in Kleene (1952: 36).

Let U be the collection defined by (9b). U is maximal, that is, contains all non-null collections.[9] By Cantor's Theorem, C(U) has a higher magnitude than U. Moreover, since U is the collection of all non-null collections, and C(U) is a non-null collection, C(U) is included in U, and is thus not larger in magnitude than U. C(U) is then both of a higher magnitude than U and yet not. This 'paradox' is only one of several related contradictions arising from free application of the notion of collection. Quine (1963: 5) sums up the situation nicely:

> The natural attitude on the question what classes exist is that any open sentence determines a class. Since this is discredited, we have to be deliberate about our axioms of class existence and explicit about our reasoning from them; intuition is not in general to be trusted here.

The paradoxes representing the 'discrediting' which Quine refers to have led to the development of various formal methods for dealing with collections without permitting the paradoxes. Starting with Russell's (1903) theory of types, distinct methods have been proposed and elaborated; for extensive discussion and comparison, see Fraenkel, Bar-Hillel and Levy (1973). The situation is characterized by Eisenberg (1971: 2–3):

> The appearance of such paradoxes as Russell's precipitated a search for a rigorous foundation of set theory which would avoid contradiction. Cantor's vague pseudo-definition of 'set' ... would no longer suffice. What was needed instead was a precisely stated system of axioms saying enough about the behavior of sets to capture the intuitive meaning of 'set' and yet, hopefully, to so delimit this concept as to avoid paradox.
> The earliest attempt to axiomatize Cantor's 'naive' theory was that of G. Frege in 1893–1903. Frege included a so-called axiom of abstraction, which asserts the existence, for any given property, of a set whose members are precisely

---

[9] Evidently, a collection that contains all non-null collections contains itself. This is perhaps odd, but not necessarily in itself contradictory. But Russell (1903) showed that it does indeed lead to a contradiction, called Russell's Paradox, which is in certain respects more fundamental than Cantor's Paradox. See Fraenkel (1966: 46–7) for discussion.

those objects having the property. Of course, Russell's paradox is an immediate consequence of that axiom.

The various axiom systems currently and widely in use by mathematicians may be divided into two kinds according to the way they resolve the difficulties of the axiom of abstraction. The first is due to E. Zermelo, A. A. Fraenkel and T. Skolem. There a given property determines only the set of those objects which have the property and which are also members of some set already known to exist. Thus the Zermelo–Fraenkel–Skolem system simply prohibits the formation of such gigantic collections as Russell's $\mathcal{R}$.

The second kind of system is due essentially to J. von Neumann, P. Bernays, and K. Gödel. Here the primitive notion corresponding to the intuitive idea of a collection of objects is that of a *class*. The axioms specify the behavior of classes. A *set* is by definition a class which is a member of some class. For a given property, one is guaranteed the existence of a class whose members are exactly those classes which are actually sets and which have the property. Russell's collection turns out to be a class which is not a set.

We will adopt, although entirely informally, the general viewpoint of the second approach to set theory, one distinguishing class and set. We use, however, the term 'collection' rather than 'class', because current usage strongly tends to take 'class' and 'set' as completely interchangeable. Our notion of a collection is then simply the extension of an arbitrary condition. Within the framework adopted, every set is a collection but not conversely. It is taken as a priori open whether any particular collection is a set, that is, whether it is an element of any other collection. The collections defined by (9a, b) turn out not to be sets. Consequently, some conditions do not define sets.

The problem leading to a distinction between collections and sets arises only with respect to 'very large', in fact, maximally large, collections like the collection of all sets, the collection of all cardinal numbers, etc.; see Fraenkel (1966: 51–2). More precisely, as observed by Eisenberg (1971: 52), the totality of all collections is partitioned into two subtypes, sets, and collections with the size of the collection of all sets ('the universal class'). The latter are now generally called *proper classes*, a notion apparently first introduced into formalized set theories by von Neumann (1925),[10] although he did not use this term; see von Neumann (1967). Hence every collection is either a set or a proper class. To keep our terminology consistent, we use the term *megacollection* as an equivalent for 'proper class'.[11] Megacollections then include the collections determined by both (9a, b) and all and only those which are equinumerous. See Fraenkel, Bar-Hillel and Levy (1973: especially 136–7).

No known contradictions arise from reference to mega-collections, as long as they are not confused with sets, that is, as long as they are not taken as elements of other collections. This is crucial for what follows because we not only adopt the terminological equivalent of proper classes but also the basic attitude toward them introduced by von Neumann and described as follows by Fraenkel, Bar-Hillel, and Levy (1973: 137):

> Thus classes, or at least proper classes are regarded as a kind of objects different from sets, and in some sense less real than sets. On the other hand, von Neumann's motivation regards classes and sets as objects of the same kind with the same claim for existence. The only difference between proper classes and sets is that, because of the antinomies, the proper classes cannot be members of classes whereas sets can.

Because we adopt, and show in chapter 4 that one must adopt, a set-theoretical framework which appeals to megacollections, it is important to observe that there are no serious set-theoretical grounds for rejecting such a move. Many formalized set-theories

---

[10] However, the distinction between collections which are proper classes and those which are sets was known to Cantor, as revealed, for example, in his letter to Dedekind of 1899, reprinted in translation as Cantor (1967), in which one reads (114): 'If we start from the notion of a definite multiplicity ... (a system, a totality) of things, it is necessary, as I discovered, to distinguish two kinds of multiplicities ... For a multiplicity can be such that the assumption that *all* of its elements "are together" leads to a contradiction, so that it is impossible to conceive of the multiplicity as a unity, as "one finished thing". Such multiplicities I call *absolutely infinite* or *inconsistent multiplicities*. If on the other hand the totality of the elements of a multiplicity can be thought of without contradiction as "being together", so that they can be gathered together into "*one* thing", I call it a *consistent multiplicity* or a "set".' Moreover, in this letter, Cantor indicated that the collection of all cardinals was a proper class.

[11] Our megacollections are also equivalent to Quine's (1963: 3) *ultimate classes*.

only permit characterization of sets, and it might even be correct
to say that these are more standard. There is not, and probably
cannot be, any finitary proof of the consistency of minimally
strong set-theories; see Beth (1959: 495), Fraenkel, Bar-Hillel and
Levy (1973: 325). However, if the 'standard' set-theories which
exclude proper classes are consistent so is, for example, that of
von Neumann (1967), which incorporates them; see Fraenkel,
Bar-Hillel and Levy (1973: 132), Quine (1963: 319). Consequently,
in itself, introduction of the notion of proper classes (collections
too extensive to consistently be taken as sets) determines no
inconsistency. Thus, if, as we show in chapter 4, linguistics must
be based on a set-theoretical framework which permits appeal to
proper classes, this is as safe from contradiction as appeal to more
familiar set-theories, which do not.

Because of the necessity of restricting the possibility for collections to be elements, our earlier account of Cantor's Theorem,
stated in terms of collections, is not strictly correct. In particular,
the power collection of a megacollection W is *not* larger than W.
The account becomes unimpeachable when described, as it standardly is, as holding of sets.[12] In these terms, it is a truth about an
arbitrary set and the collection of all of its subsets, called its *power
set*. Cantor's Paradox is then interpretable as showing that there is
no set of all sets; see Halmos (1960: 10–11). Put differently, it
shows that given any set, one can always find a bigger one,
namely, its power set.[13] As Gödel (1964: 263) states:

> It follows at once from this explanation of the term 'set' that
> a set of all sets or other sets of a similar extension cannot
> exist, since every set obtained in this way immediately gives

[12] Actually, as Eisenberg (1971: 221) observes, part of Cantor's Theorem is valid
for all collections.

[13] One might wonder whether Cantor's Paradox is avoidable by denying that
certain sets have power sets. The existence of such sets is suggested by the
intuitive character of the definition of 'power set' together with the extensional
nature of sets. It is guaranteed in formal accounts by an explicit axiom; see the
discussion of Halmos' Axiom of Powers in section 4.3. It is pointless to block
Cantor's Paradox via an ad hoc limitation on power sets, since e.g. Russell's
Paradox arises independently of power sets, and shows that the real source of
inconsistency is more deeply embedded in traditional assumptions about collections and is independent of power sets. Moreover, devices which suffice to block
Russell's Paradox suffice to block Cantor's, without denying that every set has a
power set.

rise to further applications of the operation 'set of' and, therefore, to the existence of larger sets.

While there is thus no end of sets and no set big enough to encompass all sets, there is a collection of all sets, but it is a megacollection, not a set. Correspondingly, since some collections are not sets, there is no collection of all collections. In so far as a collection does form a set, then (i) it can be an element of other collections (sets) and (ii) has a fixed power (finite or transfinite). Thus one can assign a fixed cardinality to the collection of all positive integers; this is the power Cantor referred to as $\aleph_0$; another, $2^{\aleph_0}$, is assigned to the continuum, another $2^{2^{\aleph_0}}$, to the power set of the continuum, etc., yielding an infinite sequence of successively greater infinite magnitudes. But there is no point in this hierarchy which gives the magnitude of megacollections, no cardinality to a collection the size of one containing all sets ... there are just too many of them to (even transfinitely) count.

One implication of the previous discussion is particularly important. Sets are fundamental to every branch of mathematics and formal study. Indeed, it is sometimes said that all mathematical objects are sets. So it is crucial to be able to characterize them. But the total universe of sets provably does not itself form a set. Nonetheless, set-theoretical work has provided vast and deep knowledge of sets and a rich characterization of them. Consequently, one must avoid the unwarranted conclusion that the fact that there is no set encompassing all of some domain prevents a theoretically viable and insightful account of that domain. Taking the platonist view that abstract objects like sets are real (see Katz (1981; 1983)), there are fundamental aspects of reality which can be seriously characterized, although they are too vast to be encompassed by any single set. Since this is the case for several aspects of the reality studied in logic and set-theory, it could hardly be tragic or even surprising if it also turned out to be the case in other domains.

1.3   NLs, collections and sets

Of what, if any, relevance could the problems of sets and collections be for linguistics in general and grammatical theory in particular? Their significance is that collections studied in linguistics might have the same magnitude as those specified in (9), that is, they might be megacollections. In particular, collections defined by conditions such as those in (10) could be of this order:

(10)   a.   x is an English (Mongolian, etc.) sentence
         b.   x is an NL sentence
         c.   x is an NL

Determining the nature and hence the magnitudes of collections like those defined in (10) is a fundamental linguistic issue. At a minimum, a grammatical theory must[14] characterize the collection satisfying (10c); that is, the theory should say what NLs are and how they differ from other entities such as carrots, sonatas and integers. Thus one thing which investigation of NLs must determine is whether collections like those determined in (10) are sets.

Despite this, until now, there has been little or no discussion of such matters. Questions about the magnitude of collections like those specified in (10) have essentially been begged. This question begging has had two aspects. First, it has been assumed without argument that, e.g. the collection of English sentences is a set, and second, that this set is countably infinite. The only objections to the first assumption that have been raised concern the possibility that the collection of sentences of an NL cannot be *precisely* characterized, that it constitutes a 'fuzzy set' (Hockett (1968); Scott (1973); Zadeh (1965)); this objection is irrelevant to our concerns.[15] Discussion of the second assumption has been limited to the question whether the collection of NL sentences is in fact finite (Hockett (1968)). Fuzziness aside, if the collection is finite, it is a set. However, the overwhelmingly dominant view since it was introduced into linguistics by Chomsky's works of the mid 1950s is that collections like that in (11a) are *countably* infinite sets.

---

[14] We also hold, following Katz (1981; 1983) and Johnson and Postal (1980), that grammatical theory proper is concerned with no more than this. In particular, a grammatical theory is not a theory of human language learning or any other psychological/biological domain, as claimed in the Chomskyan tradition. See chapter 6.
[15] Chomsky (1980a: 126–7; 1981a: 4; 1981b: 4–5) also seems to raise this objection, by asserting that languages are 'epiphenomena', or that it is unclear that there are such things. See section 6.4.

Strikingly, examination of the linguistic literature reveals that this doctrine has been supported in only one limited aspect: it has been argued that the collections in question are not finite (see section 3.2). But this conclusion does not even begin to determine that NLs are countably infinite sets. It is consistent with their being sets of any higher transfinite order, or, with their being collections like those defined by (9) *that are not sets at all.* The literature contains absolutely nothing, however, which supports the decision that individual NLs are countably infinite sets rather than one of the *infinitely many* other logically incompatible conclusions as to NL magnitude consistent with their not being *finite* sets.

2

The Received Position about NLs and their Grammars

2.1 NLs and grammars

It is important to examine the accepted generative linguistic position about collections like those represented in (10) of chapter 1, which turns out to offer no justification for the view it assumes. As presented, this standard doctrine involves not only question begging but explicit falsehoods inconsistent with Cantor's results about the hierarchy of sets and obviously illegitimate conclusions about the necessity of formulating grammars of certain sorts. The major direct consequences of decisions as to the character of collections like those in (10) of chapter 1 involve the nature of grammars. Chomsky (1959: 137), in a quite typical passage, states:

> A language is a collection of sentences of finite length all constructed from a finite alphabet (or, where our concern is limited to syntax, a finite vocabulary) of symbols. Since any language L in which we are likely to be interested is an infinite set, we can investigate the structure of L *only through the study of the finite devices (grammars) which are capable of enumerating its sentences.* (our emphasis)

Anyone familiar with the course of generative linguistics over the last quarter century will recognize that these assumptions have become absolutely standard. They deserve then close scrutiny.

The quoted passage makes the following distinguishable claims:

(1) a. An NL, e.g. English, can be regarded as a collection of sentences, taking these as formal objects of some type.

b. The collections referenced in (1a) are sets.
c. These sets are countably infinite.
d. Each sentence is a finite object.[1]
e. Each NL involves a finite vocabulary.
f. For every X, if X is an infinite set, then X can be characterized ('studied') only via finite devices that enumerate X. In the case of an NL, the finite device in question is the grammar of that NL.

Principle (1a) states that an NL can be regarded as a collection of formal objects. With this, we are in absolute agreement. Beyond (1a), we see no reason to accept the claims in (1).[2] The assertions that the relevant collections are countably infinite sets, that each sentence is finite and that the vocabulary is finite are hardly self-evident truths. More precisely, they surely have no greater self-evidence than the *false* pre-Cantorian views that every condition defines a set, that no magnitude is greater than that of the set of positive integers, etc. But Chomsky provided no arguments for any of them, and, to our knowledge, no one else has since really done so either. We return to these assumptions below.

But let us immediately consider (1f). There is a certain historical irony in Chomsky's claim, often repeated, e.g. (1980a: 221), that NL grammars are finite. For most sketches of the form of grammars he has proposed are such that the grammars of attested NLs such as English would contain an infinite number of rules. Chomsky's grammars could not be directly displayed but would have to be given finite characteristics via finite *metagrammars* or

---

[1] Chomsky does not exactly state this, claiming only that each sentence is of finite *length*. Logically, sentences could be of infinite size in some sense while still such that their (surface) length was finite. But Chomsky's intention was clearly to restrict NL sentences to finite size along all dimensions. This is, moreover, entailed in Chomsky (1965: 31), where it is specified that the collection of *structural descriptions* is enumerable. Johnson and Postal (1980) required that sentences be finite objects in a distinct way, by limiting their reconstruction of 'Sentence', called *Pair Network*, to a finite number of arcs. See footnote 5 of chapter 3.

[2] The idea that the vocabulary of NLs is finite is linked to notions of constructive grammars and its motivation seems to vanish when grammars are taken as non-constructive. See chapter 3.

hypergrammars[3] generating infinite numbers of actual grammatical rules.

First, Chomsky's current approaches to grammar all appeal to entities variously specified as 'Move NP' or, more generally, 'Move α', 'α' being a variable over grammatical categories. These are uniformly referred to as rules, sometimes as transformations, it often being said that they have permitted a reduction in the number of transformations. But, since transformations were defined as single-valued mappings in Chomsky (1955) (see also (Chomsky (1977b: 168)), there were and remain $\aleph_0$ of them in any grammar using this notion. Chomsky (1955) had an explicit terminology for distinguishing the members of the infinite set of transformations from the finite rule schemata which characterized them. The former were called *transformations*, the latter *families of transformations* (see Chomsky (1975: 381–3)). The terminology of families has been abandoned by Chomsky, perhaps for reasons sketched in Chomsky (1977b: 168).

Terminology aside, however, Chomskyan grammars have in general not been finite. Independently of the schematization of transformations, this is true because of the need to schematize phrase structure rules to allow for the unbounded possibilities of 'flat' or non-hierarchical coordination; see Chomsky (1965: 224). The strongest condition Chomsky-style grammars have in general met is then that of being finitely representable.[4]

---

[3] For discussions of the metagrammar/grammar distinction, see Langendoen (1976, 1982), Gazdar (1981a, 1982), Gazdar and Pullum (1981) and Pullum (1982).

Metagrammars have been used in particular to enumerate the rules that provide for unbounded degrees of branching in coordinate structures, for which standard phrase structure approaches require an infinite number of rules (see Langendoen (1976)). That the unboundedly long 'flat' structures of coordination require transfinitely many ordinary phrase structure rules was apparently first noted by Lees (1960b), who incorrectly claimed that this need was eliminated by Chomsky's introduction of generalized transformations. However, any finite set of such transformations would yield a finite upper bound on the number of parallel conjuncts. The only constructive approach to this problem which avoids rule schemata entirely is that of Langendoen (1978), which depends on a non-standard interpretation of phrase structure rules. In a non-constructive approach (see Johnson and Postal (1980: chapter 14)), unbounded coordination is an immediate consequence with no special statements or metastatements.

[4] On these grounds alone (see section 6.4), it makes no sense for Chomsky to claim (1981b: 4–5) that NLs are not real but that grammars are because they are represented in brains. The relation between a finite metagrammar and the infinite

From the supposed entailment in (1f), Chomsky concluded that grammars must be some subtype of Turing machine (1959: 138): 'The weakest condition that can significantly be placed on grammars is that F be included in the class of general, unrestricted Turing machines.' Not only has nothing Chomsky ever said supported (1f), it is obviously insupportable. This claim could only be true if all infinite sets were countably infinite, and hence *capable* of enumeration, a prejudice shown to be false by Cantor's work. Chomsky himself accepted (1956: 3) the existence of sets greater in magnitude than countably infinite. Since some infinite sets are not countably infinite (and some collections are not even sets), the inference that grammars must be devices which *enumerate* sets is false. Further, since Turing machines can only characterize countably infinite sets, if NLs are 'bigger' than countably infinite, their grammars are provably *not* Turing machines, the basis of the proof having already been partly provided by Cantor.

Given some non-finite collection, one can demand a finite characterization. One such type is a finitistic, proof-theoretic or *constructive* system, a Turing machine. There are now numerous general characterizations of such systems; see Boolos and Jeffrey (1974), Chomsky (1963), Gross (1972), Lewis and Papadimitriou (1981) and Wall (1972). Such devices consist of a finite set of operations with a fixed mode of application such that after a finite number of steps any element of the set to be characterized is specified. Obviously, grammars of all the various types considered in the generative tradition introduced by Chomsky and its various offshoots are subtypes of such devices, ignoring the issue about metagrammars already mentioned.[5] The nonconstructive form of grammar developed in Johnson and Postal (1980) is, exceptionally, *not* of this type; see section 5.2.

But only the collection of recursively enumerable sets, which is

---

grammar it specifies and the relation between a grammar and the infinite collection it specifies are identical. If only metagrammars are representable, Chomsky's assumptions would determine that grammars are unreal. But since only grammars describe sentences, one then derives the epistemologically absurd consequence that human knowledge of sentences rests on something unreal.

[5] By 'Turing machine', we mean any effective procedure for enumerating the objects in some domain. The relation between such procedures and grammars is nicely summed up by Osherson and Weinstein (1982: 78–9): 'Let L be an

a proper subset of the union of the finite and countably infinite sets, can in principle have constructive characterizations, and these form an insignificantly infinitesimal subset of collections in general. Far from being necessarily true, as (1f) claims, that infinite sets can only be characterized by constructive devices, most infinite collections and even some finite collections necessarily cannot be so characterized. Finite characterizations of infinite sets in general, and obviously of megacollections, must be non-constructive.[6]

The assumption underlying Chomsky's remarks, that the infinitude of NLs *requires* that grammars be Turing machines, which is basic to the history of generative grammar, is false. This view has

---

arbitrary language (set of numbers). A *positive test* for L is a procedure P, that behaves as follows. For all numbers x:

if x ∈ L, then P, given x, operates for a finite amount of time before halting.

if x ∈ L̄, then P, given x, operates forever, cycling endlessly through closed loops.

By an application of Church's Thesis, L has a positive test if and only if some Turing machine serves as that test. If a Turing machine provides a positive test for L, we say that the Turing machine *accepts* L.

'Any positive test for L can be converted into a procedure for listing the members of L in such a way that every member of L is eventually listed, and no member of L̄ is listed. Such a listing is called a *recursive enumeration*. By Church's Thesis, any recursive enumeration can be performed by some Turing machine. A Turing machine that recursively enumerates L can be construed as a *grammar* for L. Conversely, recursive enumerations can be converted into positive tests. Thus, positive tests and grammars are intertranslatable, and Turing machines provide a normal form for each....

'If L has a recursive enumeration, then L is called *recursively enumerable* (*or r.e.*). The r.e. sets, then, are exactly those accepted by some Turing machine.'

[6] Hopcroft and Ullman (1979: 6) and Lewis and Papadimitriou (1981: 33) observe that there are more languages in the sense of sets of finite strings over a vocabulary than there are finite strings, since the former has the order of the power set of the latter. The latter state: '... so the number of possible representations of languages is countably infinite ... On the other hand, the set of all possible languages over a given alphabet – that is, $2^{\aleph_0}$ – is uncountably infinite, ...' These conclusions follow from the view that a 'representation' (= grammar) can be regarded as a string. The same relative magnitude point was made in the linguistic literature in Chomsky (1956: 3). Obviously, an analogous conclusion also holds for non-constructive grammars, so there are sets of strings lacking finite non-constructive grammars as well.

But non-constructive grammars still differ relevantly from constructive ones with respect to some countably infinite and even infinite sets. For constructive grammars cannot characterize even small finite sets of non-finite objects, while these can have non-constructive characterizations. See the text below.

been extraordinarily enticing precisely because it has fallaciously been promulgated as an inevitable feature of finite specifications of infinite collections. Beyond the quotation from Chomsky (1959) given above, this position is seen clearly in statements in other well-known works. Chomsky (1979: 125) says flatly: '... some variety of recursive function theory provides the means, in principle, to express linguistic rules.' And, in an especially clear passage, Lees (1960a: xvii) remarked:

> The most restricted goal acceptable to linguistic research would be an exact and rigorously formulated *character-ization* of the grammatical sentences of some language. This characterization is accomplished by enumeration of the sentences from a finite, iterative set of rules which we call a 'grammar' ...

Lees' first sentence here is, of course, uncontroversial. The error only arises in the second sentence, which jumps to the false conclusion that a finite, rigorous characterization of a collection must take the form of an enumeration. In the same vein, Chomsky and Miller (1963: 283) remarked:

> In order to specify a language precisely, we must state some principle that separates the sequences of atomic elements that form sentences from those that do not. We cannot make this distinction by mere listing, since in any interesting system there is no bound on sentence length. There are two ways open to us, then, to specify a language. Either we can try to develop an operational test of some sort that will distinguish sentences from nonsentences or we can attempt to construct a recursive procedure for enumerating the infinite list of sentences.

Again, the first sentence in the quote is unexceptionable, as is the second. The error arises only when it is falsely claimed that the only possible finite specifications of infinite collections are either operational tests or Turing machines. We do not understand how an operational test would differ from a Turing machine. The possibility of characterizing infinite collections in such terms is obscure and has never played a role in linguistics. Hence

Chomsky and Miller were in essence claiming that a grammar had to be a recursive enumeration.

However, the claim that the specification of necessary and sufficient conditions for membership in an infinite collection must be a recursive enumeration is a non-sequitur. One absurd consequence of this claim is that a correct characterization of the realm of sets, that is, a proper set-theory, must take the form of a Turing machine. On the contrary, use of non-constructive, intensional characterizations via satisfaction as informally described in chapter 1 is the only fully general method for characterizing collections regardless of magnitude. Therefore, not only was no argument for (1f) given by Chomsky or anyone else, none is possible. Logically, it can turn out that if a collection has a finite characterization, the latter is necessarily non-constructive. NL grammars could then turn out to be necessarily non-constructive. The argument of section 5.1 shows that this is in fact the case.[7]

The serious error in (1f) is compounded when Chomsky (1959: 138) adds: 'The former condition ... has no interest. We learn nothing about a natural language from the fact that its sentences can be effectively displayed, i.e., that they constitute a recursively enumerable set.' Quite the opposite of this claim is the case.[8] Given the falsity of (1f), to demonstrate first that NLs are sets, second that they are countably infinite sets, and third that they are recursively enumerable sets would be highly significant (and, we claim, unachievable) accomplishments. Chomsky's just quoted remark obscures the fact that no grounds were given for claiming that NLs are sets, countable infinite and recursively enumerable;

---

[7] More precisely, what is proved is that if some NL has a grammar, that grammar is non-constructive. We do not consider whether there are NLs without grammars.

[8] Such claims have again become standard assumptions. Hence Bach (1971: 4) intended nothing controversial when stating: 'The first result of Peters and Ritchie was that transformational grammars defined in the spirit of *Aspects* are weakly equivalent to Turing machines. That is to say, any language that can be defined by a Turing machine or unrestricted rewriting system can be defined by a transformational grammar and vice versa. This result is somewhat disconcerting. It shows that claiming that transformational theory provides a theory of possible natural languages is making no stronger claim than that natural languages are systems of some sort. Clearly this tells us nothing that we don't already know.' That NLs might be too big to be described by any Turing machine (or transformational grammar) is not contemplated.

and, worse, that these are substantive questions.[9] To appreciate how misleading this remark really is, consider the following alteration in which the expression 'collection' replaces 'natural language', and the expression 'element' replaces 'sentences':

(2)   We learn nothing about a collection from the fact that its elements can be effectively displayed, i.e. that they constitute a recursively enumerable set.

(2) amounts to a denial of, inter alia, the fundamental results of Cantor's work on sets, which revolutionized logical investigations and work on the foundations of mathematics. The 'translation' of Chomsky's remarks reveals them to be a determination by fiat that NLs have properties which pre-Cantorian prejudice had assumed all collections must have. *That* prejudice at least preceded proofs of its falsehood.

In Chomsky's formulation, the doctrine that NLs are countably infinite is closely correlated with the view that NL grammars are constructive. However, these ideas are logically partially independent. While the countable infinitude of NLs might ('might' for reasons discussed at the end of the following section) render constructive grammars *possible*, it would do nothing to preclude the possibility or superiority of non-constructive grammars. However, if NLs are *not* limited to countably infinite sets, only non-constructive grammars are possible.

2.2   Sentence size: introduction

While giving no justification for the correlative claims that NL grammars are constructive and that NLs are denumerable, Chomsky did logically connect these assumptions to another claim, (1d), which would render the latter true and the former thus at least *possible*. For if an NL is a collection of finite objects, in

---

[9] Certain discussions of these questions seem to suggest that the recursive enumerability of NLs is inferrable from the fact that humans have internally represented grammars. There is no possible valid argument along these lines. See sections 5.4 and 6.2.

particular, of a set of strings each finite in length, then that NL is, if not finite, countably infinite, since there are various procedures for putting it in one-to-one correspondence with the positive integers; see Boolos and Jeffrey (1974: 5), Quine (1963: 210–11). Chomsky could then have provided justification for the countably infinite assumption *if* he had given arguments for the view that each NL sentence is a finite object. Instead, he was content with mere *assertions* that this is the case, for example (1957: 13): '... All natural languages ... are languages in this sense, ... each sentence is representable as a finite sequence of these phonemes ..., though there are infinitely many sentences.' A similar position is implicit in Chomsky (1965: 31, his (14)). See also Chomsky and Miller (1963: 283). These assumptions are, of course, everywhere implicit in the resulting generative literature and, on occasion (Peters and Ritchie (1973: 53)), they are explicitly reiterated; see also Harris (1968: 205).

To our knowledge, only one argument has ever been given to support the assumption that NL sentences are all of finite length.[10] This is found in Harris (1968: 10):

> Sentences are always finitely long; we can never say whether a particular word sequence is a sentence or not until it is ended, for otherwise something might still be included in the sequence that would violate the regularities of sentencehood. But there is no upper bound to the possible length of sentences, since one can always add some clause or repeat a word, such as *very*. Hence the set of sentences, as sequences of elements in a finite discrete set, is denumerably infinite ...

However, Harris's argument is inadequate. First, it confuses epistemological questions of how one knows X with questions of the existence of X. Even if Harris were right about limitations on our ability to know that infinite sequences satisfied the regularities of sentencehood, this would not entail that there are no infinite sentences. At most it would indicate that we cannot *know* that there are infinite sentences, an entirely different conclusion. Second, Harris's remarks amount in effect to a completely unjustified limitation of the means by which one can gain knowledge about (in

---

[10] Postal (1970: 224) did suggest, albeit not very seriously, that English has no finite bound on sentence length, but offered no argument.

particular) sentences. The argument depends on the unstated and unsupportable assumption that the only way one can determine that X is a bona fide sentence is by examining it in toto. This ignores the possibility of reaching the conclusion via reasoning from finite observations or intuitions. If the logic of Harris's criticism of infinite sentences were correct, it would apply with equal force to all mathematical objects. How could one say, for example, that some (putatively infinite) set is recursively enumerable without having examined all of its members, since some collection of members might fail to manifest the properties permitting enumeration? Moreover, as noted by Ziff (1974: 520), if the logic of the criticism were correct, it would apply with equal force to *long* finite sentences. Consequently, it would lead to the view that all sentences must be short enough to actually be examined, contradicting Harris's supplementary, and surely correct, claim that NLs are infinite. It is for this reason that it is recognized in formal studies that there is no real difference between huge finite sets and infinite ones. As Stoll (1963: 6) remarks:

> In this connection one instinctively tends to differentiate between finite and infinite sets on the grounds that a finite set can be realized as an assembled totality whereas an infinite set cannot. However, a large finite set (for example, the set of books described in Section 1) is as incapable of comprehension as is any infinite set. On the basis of such examples one must conclude that the problem of how to describe efficiently a large finite set and the problem of how to describe an infinite set are, for all practical purposes, one and the same.

It follows that nothing in Harris's remarks offers any basis for concluding that NLs do not contain sentences of infinite size.

Of course, if one could justifiably show that no NL sentence could be longer than some *fixed* finite length, then every sentence would be of finite size. But the arguments that show that there are no fixed finite bounds on sentence length (see section 3.3) dissolve this line of support for the sentence-finiteness claim. Further, there is no relevant argument from logical necessity. The idea of objects of (distinct orders) of infinite size has never been shown to yield any contradiction. There are now many logico-mathematical studies of 'languages' and logics involving strings of infinite length;[11] see Karp (1964), Barwise (1968), Keisler (1971), Drake (1974) and references therein. Hence the issue of whether e.g. English sentences are of this character is a *factual* one. It cannot be determined by fiat, as in Chomsky's writings and the subsequent generative literature.[12]

[11] Of course, 'string' is standardly defined such that each instance is finite; see Hopwood and Ullman (1979: 1), Lewis and Papadimitriou (1981: 29). The claim in the text then refers to a generalization in which this length limit is eliminated. Although the finiteness limitation is entirely reasonable from the viewpoint of computer science, computability studies, etc., this says nothing about whether an analogue is a truth about NL sentences.

[12] Although Chomsky's decision that all NL sentences are finite objects was never justified by arguments from the attested properties of NLs, it did have a certain 'social' justification. It was commonly assumed in works on logic until fairly recently that the notion 'language' is necessarily restricted to finite strings. For example, this was the view taken in Rosenbloom (1950: 152), whose notion of a concatenation system strongly influenced Chomsky's early work. The same decision is found in Quine (1963: 210–11), who used it to underlie the claim that there are sets which cannot be specified by open sentences (1963: 2): 'Of course, if we can specify the class at all, we can write an open sentence that determines it; ... But the catch is that there is in the notion of class no presumption that each class is specifiable. In fact, there is an implicit presumption to the contrary, if we accept the classical body of theory that comes down from Cantor. For if it is proved that there can be no systematic way of assigning a different positive integer to every class of positive integers, whereas there is a systematic way ... of assigning a different positive integer to every open sentence or other expression of any given language.' This conclusion followed only because Quine took the notion 'expression of a language' as subject to a finiteness limitation. Chomsky was also influenced by Quine's formulations (see Chomsky (1955: II–1fn)). The relevant references to Rosenbloom and Quine are on pages 105 and 106 of the published version (Chomsky (1975)). While these historical matters may give some insight into *why* Chomsky made the decision he did, they provide, of course, no argument that finiteness is a true property of all NL sentences. Moreover, as noted in the text, there are now many developments of infinitary logic. Nonetheless, the notion that a 'language', natural or formal, necessarily involves only finite sentences continues to dominate; see the remarks of Putnam (1975a: 327) quoted in section 5.3.

Compare the absence of argument for the far more fundamental assumptions of NL sentence finiteness and NL countable infinitude with the significant literature which does consider the issue of whether NLs can be regarded as *recursive* sets. This literature makes the standard assumption that NLs are recursively enumerable but then considers substantively the question of whether they are recursive. If, as shown below, the assumption of recursive enumerability is not only unsupported but incorrect, the question of recursiveness is trivially answered in the negative. For references, see Chomsky (1980a: 120–2) and Lapointe (1977).

There is an easily overlooked relation between sentence size and the nature of grammars which is independent of the magnitude of NLs. Even a *finite* set of objects some of which are non-finite cannot be characterized by a Turing machine. Some finite sets are thus not, contrary to what is occasionally claimed (Lees (1965: 40)), recursively enumerable. For example, no Turing machine can characterize even the one-sentence 'language' consisting of the denumerably infinite string of repetitions of the symbol 'x'. But this has a trivial non-constructive characterization. Assume the notion *String*, shorn of its finiteness limitation, and the predicate *Over*, a relation between a string and the vocabulary on which it is based, and a predicate *Length*, which measures the size of strings. If the 'language' to be specified is L, the characterization in question is provided in the notation of Halmos (1960) by:

$$(3) \quad L = \{z: \text{String}(z) \land (\forall V)(\text{Over}(z, V) \to \\ V = x) \land \text{Length}(z) = \aleph_0)\}$$

Informally, (3) says that L is the set of all and only those strings over the single vocabulary item x whose length is $\aleph_0$. This is the singleton set with the single transfinite string in question. Condition (3) provides an illustration that the descriptive power of non-constructive grammars is immeasurably greater than that of any proof-theoretic system.

The over-generalization that all finite sets are recursively enumerable is an understandable error if one considers how formulations of recursive function theory and Turing machines in which 'recursively enumerable' is defined are developed. Namely, such accounts uniformly start with a conception of 'string' as a finite object. And, almost immediately, attention is restricted to sets which are sets of strings, hence sets of finite strings. If then, internal to such assumptions, it is claimed that all finite sets are recursively enumerable, this is equivalent to the true proposition that all finite sets of finite strings are recursively enumerable. But this is quite different from the false claim that every finite set of any type of mathematical object is recursively enumerable, which would mean, for example, that there is a recursive enumeration of the singleton set whose only member is the uncountably infinite set of real numbers.[13]

In summary, the non-existence of NL sentences of transfinite size has neither been demonstrated nor supported. We now turn to the question of whether their existence can be demonstrated or supported. In the absence of direct evidence that such sentences do exist, one might conclude that they do not, by a superficial appeal to Occam's razor. That is, one might claim that denial of such entities simplifies the overall realm of objects that have to be recognized and thus that no such sentences should be countenanced in the absence of positive grounds for their recognition. However, Occam's razor only applies sensibly to theories or frameworks. Chapter 3 observes that the principle of simplicity actually cuts the other way. Recognition of transfinite sentences eliminates the need for certain specific statements in grammatical theory and thus simplifies the theory, with no harmful consequences. Chapter 4 then exhibits a property of NLs (closure under coordinate compounding) that determines the existence of transfinite sentences, in fact, of NL sentences of every transfinite length.

---

[13] Those who assume that all finite sets are recursively enumerable are thinking not of finite sets per se but probably of the much narrower collection of what Fraenkel, Bar-Hillel and Levy (1973: 44) refer to as *hereditarily finite* sets. These not only have a finite number of members, but membership is also ancestrally finite; hence if x is a member of a finite set Y, x might be an infinite set, but if Y is hereditarily finite, then x can have only finitely many members, and similarly for the members of x, and the members of the members of x, and so on. Metaphorically, hereditarily finite sets are finite all the way down or everywhere, while finite sets per se are finite only at the highest level. This image becomes precise if membership is represented by means of arcs (lines) in a (directed) graph-theoretic tree, with sets (and individuals) taken as nodes and arcs taken as representing membership of lower nodes in the sets represented by higher nodes. In these terms, a finite set is a node which is the tail of only finitely many arcs, but some of these may be tails of infinitely many arcs. A hereditarily finite set defines a tree with only finitely many arcs. Obviously, only collections of finite graphs are recursively enumerable.

3

Sentence Size Bounds

3.1 Size (length) laws

Section 2.2 stressed that NL sentence size and NL magnitude are intimately linked. The sporadically defended claim that NLs are finite sets depends on the view that there is a fixed finite bound on sentence size (length). The currently totally dominant claim that NLs are countably infinite sets depends on the view that while there is no specific finite bound on sentence size, each NL sentence is finite. This Chomskyan position rejects any *finite* size (length) restriction of the form (1), which would make the collection a finite set.

(1) Each sentence is less than k elements long (k a finite positive integer).

But it imposes the *transfinite* size (length) restriction:

(2)   Each sentence is less than $\aleph_0$ elements long.

Condition (2) makes the collection a countably infinite set. Of course, these conclusions about collection magnitude only follow if the relevant length restrictions correlate with size restrictions along all dimensions, *which is assumed from this point on.*

Principles like (1) and (2) will be referred to as (*NL Sentence*) *Size* (*Length*) *Laws.* They are particular instances of claims that there is a least upper bound on sentence size. (1) is really a schematic representation of a countably infinite set of distinct size laws, one for each instantiation of the variable k as a distinct finite integer. But the collection of all possible size laws is *not* represented by the union of (1) and (2). There are also those of the form:

(3) a. Each sentence is less than $2^{\aleph_0}$ elements long.

  b. Each sentence is less than $2^{2^{\aleph_0}}$ elements long.

  c. Each sentence is less than $2^{2^{2^{\aleph_0}}}$ elements long.

Given the infinitude of possible size laws, including infinitely many of the type in (3), each restricting NL sentence size to some greater infinite magnitude, the issue of sentence size is framable generally as follows:

(4) a. Either (i) there is a size law for NL sentences, or (ii) there is not.

  b. If (ai) holds, then the size law is either one of the principles schematized by (1) or it is not.

  c. If (ai) holds, and the size law is not one of those schematized by (1), then it is either (2), or it is not.

  d. If (ai) holds, and the size law is not one of those schematized by (1), and is not (2), then it is either (3a), or it is not.

  e. If (ai) holds, and the size law is not one of those schematized by (1) and is not (2) or (3a), then it is either (3b), or it is not.

(4), of course, consists of logical truths. Their examination reveals what would have to be shown to justify the claim that a particular NL is determined by a characterization which includes *any particular size law, SL_i*. Such a conclusion would have the form:

(5)   Principle (4ai) holds and the size law is SL_i

But (5) is, of course, not logically true. To support such a conclusion, it would then have to be shown that (i) the relevant NL is governed by a size law and (ii) some argument(s) determine that the size law in question is SL_i rather than any other of the infinite possibilities, in particular, not one allowing larger sentences, hence one allowing every sentence that SL$_i$ allows plus infinitely many others.

Given (4), to support Chomsky's view, taken for granted today, that the proper size law for NLs is (2), it would have to first be argued that NLs are characterized by some size law, and second that none of the size laws schematized by (1) is correct. As previously noted, the literature has *attempted* to do the latter, in ways to which we turn presently. But, third, it would also be necessary to show that none of the infinitely many other distinct possible transfinite size laws, which would allow all the sentences that (2) allows, are correct. Some attested linguistic facts, logical or factual arguments would have to support the choice of (2) as against (3a), (3b), and each of the infinite number of other transfinite size laws. Nothing in the literature even attempts to display such support. It is because the first and third requirements here have never been met that we claimed earlier that questions of the magnitude of NLs have been begged. Over the more than quarter-century development of generative grammar, no one has presented *any* justification for the view that there is *any* proper size law for NL sentences or any argument supporting the choice of (2) over any of the infinitely many alternatives *except* those represented by (1). This means that the choice of (2) rather than (3a), (3b), etc., as the proper size law has remained from the beginning of generative grammar up to the present entirely arbitrary and unjustified.

One can, moreover, go beyond the recognition of the lack of foundation for the choice of (2) as a size law, to a much stronger conclusion:

(6) The conditions characterizing the collections which are
     NLs include *no size law at all*.

The ubiquitous claim in generative work that there is no bound on sentence length is *completely* true, not just when limited to a reading of 'bound' as finite bound. There is also no infinite bound on NL sentence size, no transfinite power which specifies the maximal number of constituents in an NL sentence (or the maximal number of elements in an NL constituent), just as there is none which specifies the maximal number of elements in a set. All NL size laws, not only (1) but also (2) and (3), are false, because they are equally artifactual with respect to the real structure of NLs.

The argument for (6) will have the following general form. The only sound grounds for rejecting all instances of (1) as proper size laws reject with equal force any choice of size greater than those allowed by (1). There is no basis for rejecting instances of (1) with very large values for k which does not equally force a rejection of (2), (3a), (3b), etc. No facts or theoretical grounds determine any particular size law, or the need for any size law at all. Size is no more an essential (defining) property of NL sentences than it is of sets or graphs (see Okabe (1980)). Set theories include no analogue of any of (1), (2) or (3). Addition of a size law complicates the characterization of NLs, and Occam's razor requires that any such complication be justified. Since this is impossible, the required conclusion is that there is no size law.

3.2   Unsound arguments against *finite* size (length) laws

Since Chomsky's early studies introduced the paradigm of generative grammar, there have been repeated attempts to support the view that there is no *finite* bound on NL sentence length, hence no finite bound on the magnitude of NLs. However, most of the arguments just do not stand up. Consider the typical attempt in Postal (1964: 246–7):

> Given any sentence we can always find a longer one by replacing some verbal phrase with a conjunction of two verbal phrases, etc. Of course, the finite and in fact rather small bound on human memory will prevent actual speech behavior from making use of more than a small finite subclass of all possible sentences. But this in no way affects the psychologically and linguistically fundamental fact that knowledge of a natural language provides a speaker in principle knowledge of an infinite set of linguistic objects. Only this assumption ... makes it possible to explain why, as the limits on memory are weakened ... speakers' abilities to use and understand sentences are extended to those of greater length.

But the final claim is clearly false. Suppose the longest sentences are determined by a size law of the form (1) with k equal to one million. Then the claimed 'extension' follows, as long as there is no evidence that people can use and understand sentences more than one million words in length. But there is no such evidence, and, if there were, one could set k equal to a bigger integer. No matter what the behavioral evidence is, there is a finite size law allowing enough sentences to encompass every sentence usable by humans or any other finite creatures. The argument form in question can thus never justify the rejection of *all* instances of (1), required to determine the conclusion that NLs are at least countably infinite in magnitude.

Chomsky has given several variants of the unsound argument just discussed, e.g. (1972a: 118) and (1980a: 221–2). The latter reads:

> Although the language generated is infinite, the grammar itself is finite ... Thus, the rules of grammar must iterate in some manner to generate an infinite number of sentences, ... We make use of this 'recursive' property of grammar constantly in ordinary life. We construct new sentences freely and use them on appropriate occasions ...

These remarks clearly suggest that the assumption that a grammar defines an infinite set is necessary to account for use of language in actual life. But this is evidently false. The sum of all real human linguistic activity across all of history has involved only a finite number of sentences and any person's linguistic activities can obviously be characterized in terms of a *finite* subset of sentences, say with a sentence length less than one thousand words.

Perhaps the view Chomsky intended to express is that there is no 'general' or 'simple' way to characterize a set *both* big enough to include all usable sentences and yet smaller than countably infinite. But a finite set including every usable sentence is defined by a partial grammar, constructive or not, of the sort which generates some countably infinite superset of the wanted set, plus a non-constructive statement, analogous to the last conjunct in (3) of chapter 2, which limits sentence length to less than one thousand. Moreover, such a non-constructive statement need not complicate the theory of grammatical rules. For it need not be stated as a rule at all but could be incorporated in grammatical theory, *exactly as Chomsky's transfinite length condition is,* as a condition on, or part of the definition of, 'string'. Grammars should then be unconstrained with respect to length, but all concatenations longer than the chosen length would not be strings, hence would fail to be sentences of any NL. Again, no argument for the infinitude of NLs along the lines of Chomsky's remarks can ever apply to every instantiation of (1), so such remarks offer no support for the claim that NL collections are greater than finite.

The same lack of force characteristizes Chomsky (1981b: 4–5):

> An obvious problem to be faced is that the language, the set of pairs (s, m), is infinite. This is not a logician's quibble. The set of sentences from which we draw in normal conversation or writing, or that we understand with no difficulty, is so vast that for all practical (let alone theoretical) purposes, we might as well take it to be infinite. And as irrelevant constraints of time and attention are removed, *we see at once that there are no bounds* to our knowledge of the sound-meaning pairing. Without any change in what we know, we can understand new and more complex linguistic expressions, in principle without limit, as constraints on time, attention, and 'computing space' are relaxed. It must be true, then, that our knowledge of language is somehow represented as a finite system of rules (a grammar) that determine the properties of the infinite number of sentences of the language. (our emphasis)

But no facts cited here are incompatible with the existence of a finite grammar incorporating a size law where k is some relatively large integer.

Another critique of (1) in general is found in Katz (1966: 121–22). Two arguments are given. One is of essentially the same character as those just criticized:

> If we do not [assume that there are infinitely many sentences], we commit ourselves to a syntactic theory that places a finite bound on the set of sentences. That is, the definition of 'sentence of L' given by this theory would say that any string of words having a certain syntactic property (shorter or equal in length to some number N) is grammatical whereas strings longer than N, regardless of their syntactic properties, are ungrammatical. Such a theory would be

unacceptable for two reasons. Suppose S is a well-formed string of words in some natural language and we increase the length in some *syntactically proper manner*, e.g., by adding an adjectival modifier to one of its nouns. Now, *ex hypothesi*, the constituent of S whose length is increased to increase the length of S beyond N, e.g., the noun to which the adjectival modifier was added, is still a well-formed constituent of its type after its increase in length. Therefore, since the rest of the sentence S is well-formed and the new constituent is both well-formed and of the type that preserves sentential well-formedness when it occupies the position the old constituent had in S, we are in the embarrassing position of having to say both that the sentence obtained from S by the increase is well-formed and that it is not well-formed because it exceeds N in length. (our emphasis)

However, the contradiction Katz develops arises from the assumption only given the emphasized stipulation that such extensions are 'syntactically proper'. But this stipulation in effect begs the question of whether there are *length-independent* proper extensions and cannot support a positive answer.

An argument essentially like Katz's is given by Bach (1964: 12–13):

... although every sentence is finite in length, there is no upper limit to the length of permitted sequences. For example, the longest English statement ever made can be extended by prefixing to it *I know that ..., I know that I know that ...*, and so on.

To get a real argument for the unboundedness of the collection of sentences requires deleting the words *ever made* from Bach's statement and replacing *the longest* by *any*. But, as in Katz's argument, this would beg the question. If there really were a finite length bound, some addition of such a 'prefix' would violate it, and one cannot preclude this possibility merely by asserting that it can always be violated.

The arguments given by Katz and Bach against the existence of a finite least upper bound on NL sentence length are, of course, non-demonstrative. One might wonder whether it would be possible to provide a demonstrative argument for this conclusion, which would in effect be nothing less than a *proof* that NLs are infinite. Such a proof would no doubt exist *if* certain traditional arguments for the existence of infinite sets were sound. For example, the renowned mathematician Richard Dedekind gave in 1888 a proof of the existence of what he called infinite systems (essentially our collections); see Dedekind (1901: 64), developing a proposal of Bolzano's. The idea is to show that the realm of all objects of thought is infinite. The purported proof assumes Dedekind's notion that an infinite collection is one for which there exists a one-to-one correspondence with some one of its own proper subcollections. The proof procedes by considering the collection of all objects of thought, call it Q, and takes as axiomatic that if q is an element of Q then so is the thought 'q is an object of thought'. Therefore, the collection of all thoughts of the form 'q is an object of thought' forms a subcollection of Q, call it Q', moreover a proper subcollection since e.g. the object of thought 'x is not an object of thought' is a member of Q but not a member of Q'. The one-to-one correspondence between Q and Q' then correlates each q with a q' (moreover distinct from q) of the form 'q is an object of thought'.

Despite Dedekind's undenied eminent mathematical standing and accomplishments, the theorem he offered, although interesting, cannot be taken as sound. As observed many times, e.g. Hilbert (1967: 131) and Fraenkel, Bar-Hillel and Levy (1973: 46), the collection Q is of the sort which yields the set-theoretical paradoxes. Moreover, a key step in the proof is the postulate that if q is an object of thought so is 'q is an object of thought'. But this amounts to an inductive step, analogous to the Peano postulate that the successor of a number is a number. It seems clear then that, as with Russell's proof of the non-finite character of the class of integers mentioned in chapter 1, Dedekind's proof cannot be constructed internal to any axiomatic set theory. This can be taken to mean there is no proof of the existence of an infinite collection. (There is, of course, also no proof of the existence of finite collections.)

We have mentioned Dedekind's proposal because it bears an evident formal relation to a basic idea of the arguments of Katz and Bach, most clearly to the form of the latter. Underlying Bach's argument is, in effect, the postulate that if S is a declarative sentence of English then so is *I know that S*, a claim entirely parallel to Dedekind's assumption that if q is an object of thought so is 'q is an object of thought'. The difference between Bach's and Dedekind's accounts, other than the choice of operator, is that Dedekind's postulate is formulated in what would, today, be called purely semantic terms, whereas Bach formulated his in terms of surface structure. But the latter is non-essential in that the argument becomes no weaker if it assumes that if S is the meaning of an English declarative sentence there is a sentence whose meaning is 'I know that S'. Clearly though, the grounds which render Dedekind's account a non-proof of the infinitude of the collection of objects of thought apply equally to arguments like Bach's.

3.3   A sound argument for the non-finite magnitude of NLs

The arguments discussed in the previous section for the non-finite magnitude of NLs are typical, and thus the support for this conclusion in the literature is quite weak. However, Katz (1966: 122) does provide the basis for a decisive argument against any instantiation of (1). Since it is important to what follows, we designate the passage as (7):

> (7)   Second, a syntactic theory in which some fixed N determines whether or not a string of words is well-formed would be unmotivated. It would lack any justifiable means of choosing the N that divides the sentences from the nonsentences. Since the infinite set of strings that is considered too long is in no way structurally different from those that are granted the status of sentencehood, the length property that differentiates such strings from those that are accepted as sentences has nothing whatever to do with the structural property of syntactic well-formedness. If N is not fixed arbitrarily, the properties that fix an N are psychological properties that derive from the fact about a speaker's perceptual faculties, memory, mortality, etc.

Let us explicate, extend and clarify the argument in (7). Suppose one is interested in studying some arbitrary attested NL, L, assumed to be a collection of sentences. An attested NL is one with speakers, hence one for which there are some *attested* sentences; these are objects which direct native-speaker intuitions have determined to be sentences. Obviously, one can only study L by considering attested sentences of L, which will, by the nature of the attestation process itself, all be relatively short. Moreover, the total number of attested sentences will also, from the nature of inquiry, obviously be finite, and in fact, relatively small. Viewed abstractly, there are then two distinct collections to be considered: L and some non-null subset of attested sentences of L. Refer to *any* one of the latter as an *inductive basis of L* (henceforth: IB(L)). Let some particular IB(L) be $IB_i(L)$.

No matter how $IB_i(L)$ is chosen, there will be a finite least upper bound on sentence size in $IB_i(L)$. To determine L from $IB_i(L)$ one must distinguish among all the properties of $IB_i(L)$ the *lawful* properties of L, those which inherently distinguish elements of L from non-elements. Since, by hypothesis, all elements of $IB_i(L)$ are members of L, they cannot manifest any property P, where P is the negation of one of the defining properties of L. Moreover, while any $IB_i(L)$ can manifest properties which are accidental from the point of view of L, if $IB_i(L)$ as a whole fails to manifest certain defining properties of L, no projection from $IB_i(L)$ will yield L. This is trivial if it is remarked that a single well-formed sentence of L is an IB(L). For some $IB_i(L)$ to be an adequate basis of projection to L, it must manifest all the defining properties of L itself. Any such $IB_i(L)$ is called an *adequate inductive basis of L*. In section 7.5, we raise the issue of the existence of NLs that lack any finite adequate inductive basis.

Inherent in the above discussion is that any particular $IB_i(L)$ is, from the point of view of L itself, arbitrary and that a projection to L will be possible, for at least some NLs, from many distinct IB(L)s, but not necessarily from any arbitrary one.

Suppose now k is the length of the longest sentence in $IB_i(L)$. A lawful characteristic of $IB_i(L)$ is then:

(8)   The length of a sentence is $\leq k$.

But clearly it would be absurd to imagine that (8) is a defining feature of L itself. Nothing inherent in L has determined the limits on any IB(L); these are in part arbitrary and accidental and in part simply a function of the conditions on human linguistic research. Moreover, obviously, various distinct IB(L)s will *differ* in their maximum sentence size, while L, whatever its boundaries, is fixed. Hence the assumption that (8) is a property not merely of arbitrary IB(L)s but of L itself will lead to contradiction.

To see further that principle (8) is a property of something distinct from L, imagine creatures, call them Woocoos, with life spans one million times greater than ours, with one billion times more memory and with comparable extra reasoning power. Clearly, the IB(L)s of Woocoo linguists studying NLs spoken by Woocoos would be subject to an entirely different and much weaker size principle than (8). Such principles thus provide no information about L but only about the process of linguistic research on L carried out by creatures with fixed limitations.

Given any particular IB(L) with maximum size bound k, the search for the lawful properties of L thus must ignore k. That is, were there any size bounds on NL sentences, these could not possibly be equated with size bounds on IB(L)s. But what about some other choice of finite upper bound distinct from k? Here, Katz's formulation (7) makes the obvious point that the non-arbitrary bases for such a choice would yield some value which would incorporate the perceptual, memory, mortality, etc. limits of the speaker. But such values derive from the (linguistically) accidental properties of speakers of L rather than from L. That is, they are performance limitations. By again imagining the non-human Woocoos mentioned just above, one would determine a distinct value. Hence the finite upper bound derived from such factors is a non-linguistic parameter (or vector of parameters) and tells one nothing about L. See also section 6.3.

Another way of putting this claim that non-arbitrary choices for least upper bounds on sentence length are actually performance limitations is to note the clear difference between any attempt to determine a value for k in (8) and attempts to determine grammatically in the standard sense. Put simply, no speaker of any NL has ever even been claimed to have any intuitions about sentense length per se. There is no case where an intuition of ill-formedness is attributable to mere length. All that is ever observed is that as sentences become longer, they become harder to understand, perform, etc. But these are performance properties independent of any NL and dependent on the properties of the creatures attemptign to understand, perform, etc. An intuition of ill-formedness truly due to length would have to involve structures which are not in conflict with performance limitations but still intuited to be ill-informed.

The absence of linguistically relevant bases for imposing finite upper bounds leaves the possibility of choosing some finite upper bound arbitrarily. But linguistic research is concerned with determining the truth about NLs and arbitrary assumptions can play no role in such a determination. It follows that the first part of what we take to be Katz's sound argument against the existence of finite bounds on NL sentence length is this. There is no basis for a non-arbitrary choice which is non-linguistic. Hence to impose a fixed finite bound on sentence size is to make either a non-linguistic choice which is redundant because anything it accounts for would follow from an independent theory of the relevant creatures or to make a choice which is completely arbitrary. Neither choice is possible for a true theory of NLs. Moreover, imposing a finite length bound at all is totally unmotivated.

However, Katz's passage (7) includes the basis for a somewhat different argument as well. Focus on the lawful properties of L, by hypothesis now successfully induced from $IB_i(L)$. Let us refer to these jointly as P. P distinguish L from other NLs, and from things which are not NLs at all. More specifically, P distinguish sentences of L from sentences of other NLs and from things which are not NL sentences at all, as follows. Something is a sentence of L if and only if it satisfies all of P, that is, meets all the conditions on sentencehood in L.

Now, pick some positive integer j which is bigger than the bound on the $IB_i(L)$ and, moreover, sufficiently large so that no sentence bigger than j is even attestable by (for) humans. Katz's passage (7) points to the following fact. No matter how j has been chosen, there are sentences, in fact, infinitely many (even) finite sentences, which satisfy P but which are bigger than j. This follows from the assumption that P are size-independent. But since the previous argument shows that there is no non-arbitrary linguistic basis for a finite length bound, this already follows. The objects satisfying P but larger than j thus have all the properties which distinguish sentences of L from sentences of NLs distinct from L and from objects which are not sentences of any NL. It is clear then that there neither are, nor can be, any reasons for excluding them from L which could not justify excluding any sentence too big to be attestable from L. Moreover, there is no reason for excluding them from L other than their size-determined and creature-dependent unattestability which would not equally justify excluding any sentence at all from L. Once one determines, as we already have, that attestability per se is a creature-determined property of sentences independent of, and irrelevant to, their linguistic nature and irrelevant to the bounds of NLs, the argument just given establishes that the choice of any finite size bound on NL sentences necessarily excludes from the characterization of L infinitely many finite sentences which have all of the defining properties of sentences of L. Certainly though, objects having all of the defining properties of sentences of L *are* sentences of L. Hence imposition of any finite size bound on NL sentences yields a description which excludes from its characterization of L infinitely many bona fide sentences of L. But any such description is false.

Hence Katz's passage (7) contains in effect two arguments that no correct theory of NLs can incorporate finite bounds on sentence size. The first is that any choice of such bounds is either wholly arbitrary or else necessarily non-linguistic. The second is that any such bound necessarily leads to a description which excludes from the description of an NL infinitely many objects having all the defining properties of sentencehood in that NL, that is, excludes from the description infinitely many sentences of that NL.

A consequence of these arguments is that any NL contains not only infinitely many unattested sentences but infinitely many unattestable sentences, where 'unattestable' is actually a schema defining an open set of predicates depending on how one fixes the limitations of particular NL speaking creatures.

We have just seen how one can explicate passage (7) via reference to a projective property linking attested NLs to their inductive bases. We can now state this projective property more precisely via appeal to the notion *inductive collection*, defined as follows.[1] Let US be the collection of all NL sentences (see section

---

[1] See Enderton (1974: 25) for the definition of 'inductive set'. Our definition of 'inductive collection' generalizes his definition to allow for inductive mega-collections.

5.2). Let B ⊆ US be a finite set of sentences of some NL L, which is, moreover, an adequate inductive basis of L. Let F be the family of mappings of sentences of US into sentences of US that preserve the defining conditions on sentencehood in L. Let S ⊆ US be a collection of sentences that contains B and that is *closed* under the mappings in F. A collection S is closed under F if and only if, for each f in F, if x is in S, then f(x) is in S. Any such collection S we call an *inductive collection* over the pair ⟨B, F⟩. We now say that L is the intersection of all inductive collections over ⟨B, F⟩. Thus, if S is an inductive collection over ⟨B, F⟩, then L ⊆ S. It is easy to see that L is itself an inductive collection over ⟨B, F⟩ and that it is the smallest such collection since it is included in every inductive collection over ⟨B, F⟩.

We illustrate this method of speaking about attested NLs with an artificial example.[2] For simplicity, we will consider the sentences of such artificial languages to be elements of US, although of course they are not. Let L be a language whose sentences satisfy the defining structural conditions in (9).

(9)　a.　Each sentence begins with the word a.
　　　b.　Each sentence ends with the word b.
　　　c.　In no sentence can the word a be immediately followed by the word a.
　　　d.　In no sentence can the word b be immediately preceded by the string bb.

It is evident that the sentences of L include those in (10) and that all sentences in L of length seven or less are in (10).

(10)　　　　　　　　a.　ab
　　　　　　　　　　b.　abb
　　　　　　　　　　c.　abab
　　　　　　　　　　d.　ababb
　　　　　　　　　　e.　abbab
　　　　　　　　　　f.　ababab
　　　　　　　　　　g.　abbabbb
　　　　　　　　　　h.　abababb
　　　　　　　　　　i.　ababbab
　　　　　　　　　　j.　abbabab

---

[2] The description of an actual NL is, of course, beyond the scope of this study.

In giving an inductive definition of L, it is necessary to specify an adequate inductive basis B of L. Many choices can be made, but not the singleton set {ab}, since its one member fails to exhibit all the defining conditions of L (in particular, the condition (9d) on sequences of b's).[3] One can, however, take B to be the set of sentences of L of length five or less, namely, {ab, abb, abab, ababb, abbab}. The family F of mappings that preserve all defining conditions on sentencehood in L includes the mappings A, B1, and B2 defined in (11), where z is any string of words in the vocabulary of US.[4]

(11)   a.   Azbb = zbab
           b.   B1zab = zabb
           c.   B2zabab = zabbab

Included in F are mappings other than those in (11), but these can be ignored. For consider such a mapping C. If Cx = y, then if y is a sentence of L, it can also be obtained by application of the mapping in (11). If y is not a sentence of L, then the fact that it can be obtained using C is of no interest.

The sentences in (10) are included in every inductive collection over ⟨B, F⟩. Sentences (10a–e) are included by virtue of being members of B; (10f–j) are obtained from elements of B by the mappings in (11), as indicated in (12).

(12)   a.   ababab = Aababb
           b.   abbabb = B1abbab
           c.   abababb = B1Aababb
           d.   ababbab = B2Aababb
           e.   abbabab = AB1abbab

---

[3] The notion of an inductive basis and of an adequate inductive basis of an attested NL have mathematical analogues, which serve to illustrate them. Consider the Fibonacci series of positive integers, defined as follows. The first member of the series is the number 1, the second is the number 1 and each subsequent member of the series is the sum of the two immediately preceding members. Accordingly, the subsequence 1, 1, 2 is an adequate inductive basis of the Fibonacci series, and is the shortest such basis, since the subsequences 1 and 1, 1, while constituting inductive bases, are not adequate inductive bases of the series.

[4] For convenience, we omit parentheses around the arguments of the mappings; thus, $Azbb = A(zbb)$. We assume that the mappings A, B1 and B2 are identity mappings on arguments that are not mentioned in (10); for example, that $Ax = x$, where $x = zbb$.

Even if one restricts oneself to the mappings in (11), some inductive sets over ⟨B, F⟩ contain sentences that are not in L; for example, the sentence abcabab is the value of the mapping AB1abcab, and therefore is in any inductive collection over ⟨B, F⟩ which contains the set B together with the sentence abcab. However, this sentence is not in *every* inductive collection over ⟨B, F⟩, and so is not a sentence of L.

The language L is the smallest collection of sentences drawn from US that is inductive over ⟨B, F⟩. If US is taken to be a finite set, then L is a finite subset of that set. If US is taken to be a denumerably infinite set, each member of which is of finite length, then L is the denumerably infinite set of sentences that is generated by the finite-state grammar (13).[5]

(13)   a. $S \to \{A, B\}b$
                         b. $A \to (S)a$
                         c. $B \to A\ b$

The position taken in the passage (7) is in effect that NLs are countably infinite projections from their finite (adequate) inductive bases.

We take it then that Katz's passage (7), as just explicated, provides a sound basis for rejecting the existence of any *finite* least upper bound on NL sentence size, that is, refutes any instantiation of size law (1). We now consider the implications of these arguments for the currently unquestioned view that there is a *transfinite* least upper bound on NL sentence size, $\aleph_0$. In fact, both aspects of Katz's argument apply with equal force to this and, indeed, *to any possible size law*. First, any choice of transfinite size law is arbitrary and, moreover, negatively motivated, since transfinite size laws complicate the theoretical account of NLs no less than finite size laws and are equally subject to Occam's razor. Second, no transfinite size law is determined for L by any IB(L). Moreover, no matter what choice of transfinite size law is made for L, it again excludes indefinitely many objects possessing the defining properties of sentences of L and yet bigger than the limit imposed by that size law. Any transfinite size law thus also necessarily excludes infinitely many sentences from the description, and thus yields a false description.

---

[5] We leave the proof of this proposition to the reader.

To see how this consequence follows, consider the language L defined by the conditions in (9). We have already noted that if sentences of L are restricted to finite length, then L has at most denumerably many sentences. If sentences of L are allowed to be of length $\aleph_0$, it is easy to show that L has as many as $\aleph_1$ sentences and that there are sentences of length $\aleph_0$ that satisfy the defining conditions on sentencehood in L. We show this by establishing a one-to-one correspondence between a subset of L and the set of real numbers in the interval $0 \leqslant x < 1$. Let the string ababb be interpreted as the numeral 0 in the binary expansion of a real number in the interval $0 \leqslant x < 1$, and let abbab be interpreted as the numeral 1, and suppose that a decimal point is understood before the leftmost a in any sentence of L. Thus the string ababb = .0 = 0, ababb = .1, ababbababb = .00 = 0, ababbabbab = .01, abbabababb = .10 = .1, abbababbab = .11, etc. Since, by assumption, sentences of L can be of length $\aleph_0$, there is a distinct sentence of L for each real number in the interval $0 \leqslant x < 1$.

Moreover, as the length of sentences of L is allowed to increase, the cardinality of the set of sentences of L increases correspondingly. Thus, if the length of sentences of L is limited in any way, even to some fixed, *transfinite* length c, there are infinitely many sentences of length greater than c that exhibit the defining conditions of sentencehood in L. But, as stressed earlier, objects having all the defining conditions of sentencehood in an NL *are* sentences of that NL. Therefore, *any* restriction, finite or transfinite, on the length of NL sentences yields a framework unable to describe infinitely many well-formed sentences in every NL.[6] Clearly then, no such restriction can be part of any true theory of NLs. We argue in chapter 6 that this sweeping conclusion cannot be avoided by claims to the effect that underlying ontological commitments arising from a priori views of the nature of NLs and

[6] Johnson and Postal's (1980) unargued imposition of a finiteness condition on sentences by limiting each pair network to a finite number of arcs was as arbitrary and unmotivated as Chomsky's. It explained no facts and had no supporting factual consequences. Being a useless complication, it violates Occam's razor. The theory can be simplified with no loss by eliminating condition (52b) of Johnson and Postal (1980: 51) from the definition of 'R-graph', which is referenced in the definition of 'Pair Network', arbitrarily guaranteeing the finiteness of the latter.

linguistics preclude recognition of transfinite sentences. Since considerations internal to linguistics based on simplicity lead to their recognition and since Occam's razor forbids the incorporation of useless complications, the conclusion seems inescapable.

It is generally accepted today that there is no finite least upper bound on NL sentence size. We have just shown, however, that the only truly sound basis for this conclusion, namely, our development of the argument in (7), generalizes and precludes with equal force adoption of the view that there is any least upper bound on NL sentence size whatever. Hence investigation of the grounds for accepting the standard generative view that NLs are infinite collections shows these very grounds lead to the rejection of the size law in (2) and, more generally, to the rejection of all size laws. The only tenable extant basis for assuming that NLs are at least countably infinite in magnitude inevitably supports principle (6). Thus remarks like that of Chomsky (1957: 23) hold more generally than has previously been recognized: 'In general, the assumption that languages are infinite is made in order to simplify the description of these languages.' Maximum simplicity is achieved not merely by assuming that NLs are infinite but by recognizing that their sentences are subject to no size bounds at all, finite or transfinite.

We have argued that (i) there is no motivation for imposing size laws on NL sentences and (ii) since such restrictions complicate grammatical theory or individual grammars, they must be rejected. We now analyze these claims a little more deeply, to show that they are relatively independent of certain possibly controversial assumptions about the character of grammars. In particular, we want to show that the conclusion does not beg the question of whether proper NL grammars have the non-constructive ('satisfaction') form described in section 5.2.

First of all, viewed from the point of view of a *non-constructive* approach to grammars (see section 5.2), size laws yield a straightforward complication since they show up either in the definition of 'Sentence' or one of its subcomponents, or in a sentence law, or in individual grammatical rules as a statement with a form essentially like (1), (2) or (3). But the identical account with the statement simply removed is just as adequate for all known facts, and hence, via Occam's razor, the statement must be eliminated. The

Occam's razor argument is then clearly valid in non-constructive terms.

Consider then constructive approaches to grammar. There are in principle two distinct relevant varieties. One type will contain as part of its underlying formalization a definition of 'string' or its equivalent. If this definition involves, as is standard, the claim that strings are finite, this is in effect an instantiation of size law (2). This first type then directly falls under the Occam's razor criticisms already described. But suppose it is possible, as suggested by E. Keenan (personal communication), that certain constructive approaches to grammars would not involve any such stipulation about strings. This second type of constructive approach might give only the maximally general, size-independent account of string. It might be claimed that finiteness was nonetheless imposed on all sentences because of the nature of constructive systems. That is, it might be claimed that since, in a constructive system, each sentence must have a finite derivation ('proof'), such a derivation being a finite ordered set (sequence) of finite strings, a constructive system obtains the consequence that all sentences are finite 'for free', this being a theorem of its very nature. If this line of suppositions were correct, the Occam's razor argument against size laws could not apply to such systems, and it might seem that there existed the possibility of a justified inference to the claim that all NL sentences are finite.

Of course, the claim that all NL grammars are constructive entails the size law (2). But, analogously, the claim that each NL grammar involves 'proofs' with each line finite and no more than k lines, k a positive finite integer, entails one of the finite size laws covered by (1). The former entailment no more justifies size law (2) than the latter justifies the instance of (1). That is, in neither case do the restrictions on the length of 'proof' lines and the length of 'proofs' which yield the entailment come free. Each entailment requires special statements, which are analogues of the Occam's razor size law violation for non-constructive grammars.

That is, looked at formally, the notion of 'proof' or 'derivation' is simply an ordered set of strings, each string being an ordered set. Nothing inherent in this notion determines that the overall sets of strings are finite, or that each individual string is. Constructive grammars are simply that very special case of overall 'proof' systems in which *both* all strings and each set of strings forming a 'proof" are finite. The fact that constructive grammars require special statements to impose the finiteness which defines their 'proofs' may have been obscured by failures in explicitness. For example, Chomsky (1959: 142), in one of the early works introducing the notion 'derivation' into linguistics, gave a definition of 'ψ derivation of ω' as a sequence of strings $\varphi_1, \ldots, \varphi_n$, where $n > 1$. While it was clearly Chomsky's intention that n range only over finite cardinals, he did not explicitly say this, although other aspects of his axiomatization of phrase structure, e.g. his axiom 4, did explicitly limit certain sets to finite size. Clearly though, the claim that the notions of constructive grammar can determine the finiteness of sentences 'for free' is entirely false.

In a completely general proof-theoretic system, neither strings nor the sequences of strings forming proofs need be finite. Viewed historically, such systems might seem to be extensions of finite 'proof' systems; but, viewed logically, the latter are subcases of the former. In fact, systems not subject to finiteness conditions are appealed to in studies of infinitary logic, as illustrated, for example, by the following passage from Scott (1965: 332–3):

> We say that a sentence A *follows syntactically* or is *provable* from a set Φ of sentences if there is a proof of A from Φ; that is, a transfinite sequence of sentences $B_0, B_1, \ldots, B_\xi, \ldots, B_\beta$ where $\beta < \omega_1$ such that $B_\beta = A$ and for each $\xi \leqslant \beta$, the formula B_ξ is either a logical axiom, a member of Φ, or follows from previous formulas in the sequence by one of three rules of inference. There is no need to consider proofs that are non-denumerably long, since the only infinitary rule of interference makes its conclusion from only denumerably many premises.

Therefore, any claim that the finiteness restriction on NL sentences is justified by the fact that NL derivations ('proofs') are finite simply determines a regress. It now becomes necessary to justify the stipulation that NL derivations are indeed constructive and not like the proofs in e.g. Scott's infinitary logic. But the restrictions which would determine the finiteness of all 'proofs' are complications over the general characterization of 'proof', which is size-independent. Hence the regress is pointless and yields no escape from the conclusion that size laws are unjustified. These remarks apply *mutatis mutandis* to systems making use of recursive definitions as well. The standard limitation that the recursion step is applied only a finite number of times also is not obtained 'for free', and falls under Occam's razor as well.

The considerations showing that there is no size law of any sort for NL sentences yield the same conclusion for other linguistic entities including words and phrases of various types. For instance, no considerations justify any finite bound on the number of phonemes in a morphophonemic representation of a single morpheme and none suggest any transfinite bound either. In the framework of Johnson and Postal (1980), this leads to the conclusion that each NL involves an infinite vocabulary of morphemes, contradicting (Chomsky's) (1e) of chapter 2. Greenberg's (1957) notion of sign system allowed for the possibility of an infinite vocabulary, but he claimed (1957: 5) without argument that NLs fall into the subtype of sign systems with finite vocabulary.

Let us summarize the results of our investigation of NL sentence size. Largely under the influence of generative grammar, it is now universally assumed that although all attested NL sentences are relatively short, (i) there is no fixed finite bound on NL sentence size but (ii) there is nonetheless a least upper bound on NL sentence size and (iii) this bound is $\aleph_0$. Thus the position represented by (i)–(iii) amounts to a projection from small finite samples of short sentences to a countable infinitude of (finite) sentences most of which are huge beyond all conception, so huge that there are not, for example, enough protons in the known universe to put in one-to-one correspondence with their words. This standard generative position consequently already involves a theoretical recognition of entities which are not only unattested but *unattestable*. The postulation of this vast domain of entities requires arguments to justify the step from the limited corpus of experienced examples of short sentences to the countably infinite collection taken to be the NL itself.

We have found, however, that what is sound or viable in the arguments that there is no fixed, finite bound on sentence length supports the still more general and theoretically superior view that there is no bound on sentence length whatever. This leads to a recognition not only of endlessly bigger huge finite sentences but of endlessly bigger transfinite sentences as well. The idea is simply that the defining features of both NL sentencehood in general and sentencehood in particular NLs are size independent. Consequently, any limitation on sentence size, finite or transfinite, artificially excludes from characterization infinitely many well-formed sentences, and thus can only be part of a false theory of NLs. True theories must characterize all NL sentences, not just some collection whose members are arbitrarily less than one thousand, one million, $\aleph_0$, or $\aleph_\aleph$, in length. The conclusion is thus imposed that NLs are subject to no size law. This raises no new epistemological questions since the projection to a countable infinity of sentences already involves recognition of sentences which are in fact not usable, produceable, or directly knowable by humans (or even Woocoos).

But since the standard view that NLs as wholes are countably infinite sets follows only from assuming the size law (2), one must reconsider NL magnitude given that this principle can play no role in a valid grammatical theory.

4

The Analogy with Cantor's Results

4.0 Remarks

The conclusion, argued in chapter 3, that no size law is part of the characterization of NL collections raises the *possibility* that the magnitude of such collections is greater than countably infinite. We now develop a demonstration that NLs are not only bigger than countably infinite but have no determinable magnitude, that is, are megacollections. Significantly, the absence of a size law is *not* a premiss of this demonstration, but rather turns out to be a corollary of the basic NL property used to arrive at this result: *closure under coordinate compounding.*[1] To elucidate this concept, we sketch some assumptions about coordinate structures. While not necessary to the argument, these greatly simplify its presentation.

4.1 Coordination

We assume that coordinating particles like English *and*, *or*, etc., have a structure in which, quoting Gazdar (1981a: 158): '... the coordinating word forms a constituent with the immediately following node and is not simply a sister of all the conjuncts.' However, we generalize to eliminate reference to 'following' to

[1] We use 'compounding' rather than 'conjunction' to suggest that the semantic connection between the compounded elements need not be one of conjunction. It could also be inclusive or exclusive disjunction, the 'nor' relation, etc. Nonetheless, we use the term 'conjunct' to refer to the elements of compound structures.

cover NLs where the coordinating particle follows. For concreteness and ease of reference, we assume these particles belong to a grammatical category called Conj, whose elements have the following properties:

(1)   If A is a Conj node, then there exist nodes B and C such that:
    a. There is a grammatical category Q such that both B and C are Q nodes; and
    b. A is a daughter of B and the unique sister of C.

In these terms, we say that nodes instantiating variable B in (1) are *conjuncts*, while those instantiating C are *subconjuncts*. Ignoring the order of sisters, every conjunct thus has the structure:

(2)

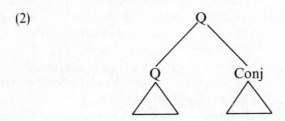

We allow a Conj terminal to be null for NLs without visible coordinating particles and for cases in NLs like English where one or more instances of Conj are not visible. Thus we take (3a) to have a structure like (3b), associating nodes with numbers for ease of reference:

(3)   a.   Tom and Bill
     b.

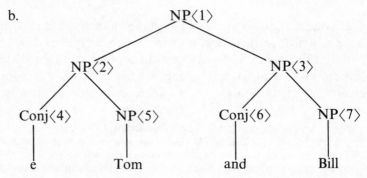

In this case, according to our definitions, nodes 2 and 3 are con-juncts, while nodes 5 and 7 are subconjuncts.

Nodes like 1 in (3b) will be referred to as *coordinate compound constituents* (*nodes*), definable as follows:[2]

(4) A constituent (node) Q is a coordinate compound of
     grammatical category C if and only if:
     a.   Q is of category C; and
     b.   Q has at least two immediate constituents; and
     c.   each of Q's immediate constituents is a conjunct.

Observe that nothing in the definition of 'coordinate compound' imposes any upper limit, finite or transfinite, on the number of immediate constituents in such structures. Coordinate compounds are evidently subject to two fundamental lawful restrictions:

(5) All sister conjuncts are of the same grammatical cate-
     gory as
     a.   each other; and
     b.   the coordinate compound constituent of which
          they are immediate constituents.

However, we take C in (4) to vary only over so-called 'major' categories, so as not to exclude the possibility of e.g. compounds of the category Plural with exclusively singular immediate constit-uents, etc.

Coordinate compounding in NLs is, we claim, governed by a fundamental condition we refer to as *coordinate compound closure*. To characterize and later use this principle, it is convenient to introduce two more basic terms.

---

[2] Obviously, (1) is not a substantively complete account of coordination. To give such, it would be necessary to make extensive substantive assumptions about NL sentence structure, which are not our concern here. In the framework of Johnson and Postal (1980), the collection of constituents of the type in question are characterized rather differently via a unique grammatical relation, represented formally by the R(elational)-sign Con. All that is necessary for the present argu-ment is that our assumptions be accurate to the extent of determining structures at least isomorphic to the correct representations of coordinate constituents.

(6) Let U be a set of constituents all of category Q and of
     cardinality >1 and let T be some coordinate com-
     pound of category Q. Furthermore, assume that:
     a. each conjunct of T has an element of U as a
         subconjunct; and
     b. each element of U is a subconjunct of some con-
         junct of T; and
     c. no element of U appears more than once as a
         subconjunct of any conjunct of T; and
     d. if two elements of U occur as subconjuncts of
         conjuncts C_i and C_j of T, then C_i and C_j occur
         in a fixed order; where C_i and C_j are of distinct
         lengths, assume the shorter precedes; where C_i
         and C_j are the same length, assume some arbi-
         trary order.
     In this case, we say both that T is a *coordinate projection
     of U* and that U is *the projection set of T*.

(6a) demands that the subconjuncts for T be drawn exclusively
from U, while (6b) demands that each element of U be used to
form some subconjunct. (6c) prevents repetitions of elements from
the projection set. (6b, c) together determine inter alia that the
number of conjuncts in a coordinate projection is identical to the
number of elements in its projection set. (6d) insures that different
orders of conjuncts are irrelevant. Given the latter, coordinate
projections of a set of constituents are unique *up to choice of
element of Conj*. For simplicity, assume the discussion is limited to
some unique element of the category Conj, thus determining a
unique coordinate projection for any set of constituents, making it
sensible to speak to *the* coordinate projection of such a set.

As stressed by E. Keenan (personal communication), it is
important to show that every subset of a collection of constituents
of category Q has a coordinate projection. But this is straightforward. For consider some such subset U. Take the cardinality of U
to be k, with k indifferently finite or transfinite. Clearly, from the
purely formal point of view, there is a coordinate compound W
belonging to the category Q, hence having immediate constituents
of the category Q. Moreover, each of these immediate constituents
is a conjunct. Since there are no size restrictions on coordinate
compounds, W can have any number, finite (>1) or transfinite of

immediate constituents. W can then, in particular, have exactly k such constituents. Each of these (conjuncts) has one and only one subconjunct. The set of all such subconjuncts, call it V, obviously then also has exactly k members. To show that W is a coordinate projection of U, it then in effect suffices that there exist a one-to-one mapping from U to V. But this is trivial, since the two sets have the same number of elements. Note that the conclusion that each subset U of constituents of category Q has a coordinate projection does not mean that the coordinate projection is necessarily well-formed in the NL from which U is drawn. The latter can only be determined by axioms to this effect, to which we now turn.

The notion of closure for coordinate compounding is as follows:[3]

(7) The Closure Principle for Coordinate Compounding:
   If U is a set of constituents each belonging to the collection, S_w, of (well-formed) constituents of category Q of any NL, then S_w contains the coordinate projection of U.

Crucially, principle (7) has a 'recursive' property in that it also refers to cases where members of U are themselves coordinate compounds.

Although not entirely clear what range of categories Q (7) holds for universally, it is, we claim, minimally valid for the one case of real concern here: where Q is the category S(entence). This yields the following instance of (7), which we take as a truth about all NLs:

(8) Closure under Coordinate Compounding of Sentences:
   a. If U is a set of constituents each belonging to the collection, S_w, of (well-formed) constituents of the category S of any NL, then the coordinate projection of U belongs to S_w.

[3] How principle (7) is formally represented in an adequate grammatical theory is important but not relevant to the present argument. It would have the logical status of what is called a *corpus law* in Johnson and Postal (1980: chapter 14); see section 5.2.

More formally and more precisely, the principle in question can be stated as follows:

b. Let L be the collection of all members of the category S of an NL and let CP(U) be the coordinate projection of the set of sentences U. Then: $(\forall U)(U \subseteq L \rightarrow CP(U) \in L)$.

Note that the phrasing 'the coordinate projection of U' is legitimate in that we have shown that U has a coordinate projection, and our subsidiary assumptions trivially (though non-essentially) determine uniqueness.

Principle (8) is no doubt too general in one respect. Sentences (clauses) fall into types: declarative, interrogative, imperative, etc. And a coordinate compound is in general only freely permitted for members of a single type. One could amend (8) appropriately, by restricting the members of U to a single type. We ignore this irrelevant complication in the wording of what follows.

We take S to be the category corresponding to well-formed independent sentences. More precisely, if a constituent Q is a member of the category S of some NL, L, and Q is not an immediate constituent of any other constituent, then Q is a well-formed independent sentence of L.

The principle of closure for coordinate compounding of sentences formalizes the following observation about collections of attested NL sentences. Given any set of Ss (of the same type), there is a well-formed coordinate compound of those Ss. Let a double arrow mean that the sentence on its right is the coordinate projection of the set of sentences on its left. Then for English:

(9) a. {Gregory is handsome; It is raining; Figs can kill; Most Slavs are morose} $\Rightarrow$

b. Gregory is handsome, it is raining, figs can kill and most Slavs are morose.

c. {a.; b.} $\Rightarrow$

d. Gregory is handsome, it is raining, figs can kill, most Slavs are morose and Gregory is handsome, it is raining, figs can kill and most Slavs are morose.

As (9d) illustrates, many of the resulting coordinate compounds are partially redundant or such that their conjuncts are totally unrelated. We thus reject the occasional suggestion (see Lakoff (1971)), that the constituent sentences of a coordinate compound sentence must, for well-formedness, have a 'common topic'. We see no reason whatever to believe that such requirements are anything other than rhetorical.

4.2 The Cantorian analogue

Let L be an NL whose vocabulary contains the name Z of a particular person or elephant. Assume L contains a denumerably infinite set, S_0, of *non-compound* sentences, each of which is about the entity Z, named by Z. This assumption seems uncontroversial, since, for many known NLs, it is easy to effectively specify such a set.[4] For example, if L is English, S_0 could be identified with a set like that implicit in the argument in section 3.2 from Bach (1964), that is, S_0 can be identified with the set in (10), where $Z = $ Babar.

(10)   {Babar is happy, I know that Babar is happy, I know
         that I know that Babar is happy, I know that I
         know that I know that Babar is happy, ...}

Assume that L is closed under coordinate compounding of clauses, that is, obeys (8). Then L also contains a set S_1 made up of all of the sentences of S_0 together with all and only the coordinate projections of ⟨every subset of S_0 with at least two elements⟩, that is, with a set containing one coordinate projection for each member of the power set of S_0 whose cardinality is at least 2. The clumsy bracketed expression arises from the fact that coordinate projections, given the nature of coordination, require by definition at least two subconjuncts, while power sets contain singletons as well as the null set. To simplify the discussion, we use the notation *>1 power set of X*, meaning that proper subset of the power set of the set X containing all and only the power set elements of cardinality 2 or greater.

---

[4] If there is an NL in which it is impossible to find denumerably many non-compound sentences each containing the name of some specific person or elephant, e.g. one lacking sentential complements, the analogy we develop could still be made. One would merely start with finitely many such sentences and let S_0 be a denumerable set of sentences consisting of the original finite set together with all finitely long coordinate compound sentences of L based on that original set.

To illustrate the construction, if S_0 is as in (10), then S_1 can be taken as the set:[5]

(11)   {Babar is happy; I know that Babar is happy; I know that I know that Babar is happy; ...; Babar is happy and I know that Babar is happy; Babar is happy and I know that I know that Babar is happy; ...; Babar is happy, I know that Babar is happy, and I know that I know that Babar is happy; ...}

The total collection in (11) is based on only seven distinct words.

By assumption, the cardinality of S_0 is $\aleph_0$. To determine the cardinality of S_1, one can observe a basic Cantorian analogy. Each member of S_1 can be put into one-to-one correspondence with a non-null member of the power set of S_0, determined as follows. Each non-compound sentence of S_1 corresponds to the singleton set whose unique element is the corresponding sentence of S_0. Each coordinate compound sentence of S_1 corresponds to its projection set. Hence each compound sentence of S_1 with two conjuncts corresponds to the set made up of the corresponding pair of sentences of S_0, each compound sentence of S_1 with three conjuncts corresponds to the set made up of the corresponding triple of sentences of S_0. Similarly, for each finite subset of S_0 of cardinality > 3, there is a corresponding compound sentence of S_1, namely, the coordinate projection of that subset of S_0. Finally, each infinite subset of S_0 also corresponds to a compound sentence of S_1, although, of course, each such coordinate projection *is of transfinite length*. At this point, conclusion (6) of section 3.1 indicating the non-existence of any size law for NL sentences, becomes relevant. See below and also chapter 6. Overall then, each coordinate compound sentence of S_1 corresponds to a member of the > 1 power set of S_0. Since the cardinality of the power set of any denumerably infinite set, and hence of S_0, is of the order of the continuum, that is, $2^{\aleph_0} = \aleph_1$,[6] the cardinality of S_1 is $\aleph_1$. Further, since L is closed under coordinate compound-

---

[5] In (11), a semicolon is used to separate the elements of a set, since commas are used as punctuation marks within those elements.

[6] Our notation assumes, purely for convenience, the 'generalized continuum hypothesis' (see Drake (1974: 65)), according to which $2^{\aleph_\alpha} = \aleph_{\alpha+1}$ for all α.

ing, the sentences of S_1 are all contained in L, and therefore, if L has any determinate magnitude, this must be of *at least* the cardinality $\aleph_1$.

To be a little more precise, in the notation of Halmos (1960), S_1 is characterizable as follows, where '$\cup$' is the sign for set union and ' $\subseteq$ ' the sign for set inclusion (subset):

(12) $$S_1 = S_0 \cup K_0,$$

where $K_0 = \{x: (\exists y)(y \subseteq S_0 \wedge x$ is the coordinate projection of y)\}.

In other words, S_1 is the union of S_0 and the set K_0 consisting of all and only the coordinate projections of the >1 power set of S_0.

Because of different possible bracketings, many coordinate compounds formed of elements of S_0 are not in S_1, because they would involve compounds whose immediate constituents are not conjuncts with subconjuncts that are elements of S_0. Alongside the 'flat' structure (13a), there are also the distinct more hierarchical structures in (13b, c), where A represents *Babar is happy*.

(13) a. $\langle\langle A \rangle$ $\langle$and I know that A$\rangle$ $\langle$and I know that I know that A$\rangle\rangle$

      b. $\langle\langle A \rangle$ $\langle\langle$and I know that A$\rangle$ $\langle$and I know that I know that A$\rangle\rangle\rangle$

      c. $\langle\langle\langle A \rangle$ $\langle$and I know that A$\rangle\rangle$ $\langle$and I know that I know that A$\rangle$

The massive number of examples like (13b, c), increasing with the number of conjuncts, are irrelevant to the discussion because we characterize collections like S_1 in terms of coordinate projections, whose relevant subconjuncts are drawn from fixed sets.

The cardinality of S_1 exceeds that of S_0 precisely because it contains sentences with transfinitely many coordinated constituents, that is, sentences violating size law (2) of chapter 3. The cardinality of the set S_0' made up of the union of S_0 with all those sentences of S_1 with at most finitely many conjuncts as immediate constituents is also $\aleph_0$. But the set S_1', the union of all of the sentences of S_0' together with the coordinate compound sentences of L whose immediate constituents are conjuncts with only sentences of S_0 as subconjuncts, is of the cardinality $\aleph_1$.

Thus, an NL not subject to a sentence size law and governed by

(8) contains at least as many sentences as the continuum. But it evidently must contain even more. Consider the union of S_1 and a set containing the coordinate projection of every member of the >1 power set of S_1. That is, consider the set S_2, definable analogously to S_1 in (12):

$$(14) \qquad\qquad S_2 = S_1 \cup K_1,$$

where $K_1 = \{x : (\exists y)(y \subseteq S_1 \land x$ is the coordinate projection of y)\}.

Via the procedure outlined for S_1, the members of S_2 can be put into a one-to-one correspondence with the members of the power set of S_1, excluding the null set. Hence the cardinality of $S_2 = 2^{2^{\aleph_0}} = 2^{\aleph_1} = \aleph_2$. Further, since L is closed under coordinate compounding, S_2 is also included within L. Consequently, the magnitude of L, if determinate, is at least of the cardinality $\aleph_2$.

Just as Cantor showed for power sets in general, the possibility of forming greater and greater sets of NL sentences always remains. For any set of sentences like S_1, S_2, etc., there is always a still bigger set *included in L*, given by the schematic characterization (15):

$$(15) \qquad\qquad S_i = S_{i-1} \cup K_{i-1},$$

where $i > 0$ and where $K_{i-1} = \{x : (\exists y)(y \subseteq S_{i-1} \land x$ is the coordinate projection of y)\}.

At no point can a set of sentences be obtained that exhausts an NL having sentence coordination governed by the closure law (8). Naturally, this will not be less true if one begins, more realistically, with *all* of the finite sentences of that NL, not just an artificially small subset of these like (4) containing only expressions sharing a single name. To prove that no set of sentences can exhaust an NL, it suffices to construct an analogue of Cantor's Paradox *from the contrary assumption*, a construction which previous remarks make directly possible. We call this result the *NL Vastness Theorem*:

(16)   THEOREM: NLs are *not* sets (are megacollections).
       Proof:
       Let $\#X$ be the cardinality of an arbitrary set X and let
       L be the collection of all sentences of some NL.

a. Assume to the contrary of the theorem that L is
    a set.

b. Then L has a fixed cardinality, $\#L$.

c. Since L is closed under coordinate compound-
    ing, L contains a subset consisting of all and
    only the coordinate projections of the >1
    power set of L. Moreover, each member of
    the >1 power set of L has a coordinate pro-
    jection. Hence $(\exists Z)(Z \subseteq L)$, where $Z = \{x:$
    $(\exists y)(y \subseteq L \wedge x$ is the coordinate projection of
    $y)\}$.

d. Since many sentences in L, in particular, all
    those elements of L which are not coordinate
    compounds, are *not* in Z, Z is a *proper* subset
    of L. That is, not only $Z \subseteq L$ but in fact
    $Z \subset L$.

e. Hence, $\#Z \leqslant \#L$.

f. But $\#Z$ is, given the definition of Z in c., of the
    order of the power set of L.

g. Hence, via Cantor's theorem, $\#Z > \#L$.

h. Since conclusion g. contradicts conclusion e.,
    assumption a. is false.

The assumption that L is a set, hence a collection having a fixed
cardinality, yields a contradiction and is thus necessarily false.
Therefore, the collection L is not a set. But L in (16) was arbitrarily chosen. Just as Cantor's Paradox shows there is no single
set containing all non-null sets, (16) shows that an NL can be
identified with no fixed set of sentences at all, no matter how great
its cardinality. Like the collection of all sets, an individual NL
must be regarded as a megacollection.

4.3 The mathematical argument as a linguistic
argument

Having constructed the central argument of this study, we now
comment briefly on its character. The demonstration in (16) that
NLs are not sets but megacollections has, like any attempt to

apply a mathematical result to some domain of facts, two distinguishable aspects. There must, first, be a proof of the relevant theorem, a question of formal mathematics, involving a purely demonstrative argument and, second, an argument, in general necessarily non-demonstrative, that the relevant domain of facts manifests all crucial properties of the mathematical assumptions underlying the proof of the theorem. For the NL Vastness Theorem, the first aspect is a rather straightforward proof that a collection of objects involving coordinate compound structures governed by the general closure principle (8) is a megacollection. We take this to be an elementary mathematical fact, closely corresponding to proofs of Cantor's Paradox and to proofs that the collection of all cardinal numbers is not a set (Eisenberg (1971: 310)). The second aspect, the consequence that this formal proof 'applies' to NLs, involves the claim that NLs do indeed model a system of mathematical objects having the properties which yield the NL Vastness Theorem. Only by confirming the second aspect of the argument can one avoid the problem properly noted by Hockett (1966: 186): 'An ironclad conclusion about a certain set of "languages" (in the formal sense) can be mistaken for a discovery about real human language.'

There is another way to put the point. As with any proof from assumptions A to a conclusion Z, one can regard the NL Vastness Theorem as a proof of the conditional $A \to Z$. This proof does not require that A be true. But the detachment of Z as a true consequence then only follows via Modus Ponens, which requires that the antecedent of a conditional be true. Therefore, (16) is a proof of a conditional whose consequent is the conclusion that NLs are megacollections. But to derive the actual non-conditional conclusion, that is, the NL Vastness Theorem itself, via Modus Ponens requires that the antecedent be true. In effect, this antecedent is the claim that NL coordination is governed by the closure principle (8). Surely, skepticism about the NL Vastness Theorem must focus on this axiom, which is not a traditionally or currently accepted linguistic principle.

Let us therefore briefly refocus attention on condition (8), the claim that NLs are closed under the coordinate compounding of sentences. Although not a familiar principle of past or present linguistics, (8) expresses, we claim, a profound truth about NLs. It says not only that the principles of grammatical theory and the rules of grammar directly relevant to characterizing coordinate structures must not themselves preclude closure, but that no other rules can have this effect. No matter how one characterizes the collection of coordinate structures of English, closure would be violated if some *independent* English rule said, for example, that there was a maximum bound on number of conjuncts, or one which said that some particular pair of clauses could not form a coordinate compound, etc.[7] Similarly, (8) would be violated if some rule of English required every coordinate compound to have *more* than k conjuncts for some fixed k. But the known facts about coordinate compounding in NLs reveal the existence of no such constraints. Principle (8) claims that the lack of such is non-accidental.

Closure principle (8) plays a role in the proof of the NL Vastness Theorem analogous to that played in set-theoretical discussions by axioms which determine that every set does have a power set. For instance, Halmos (1960: 19) writes:

> We have been considering the subsets of a set E; do those subsets themselves constitute a set? The following principle guarantees that the answer is yes. *Axiom of Powers* For each set there exists a collection of sets that contains among its elements all the subsets of the given set.

See also the Axiom of Subsets in Eisenberg (1971: 71). These axioms guarantee that the collection of sets is closed under power setting in essentially the way (8) guarantees that the collection of sentences of an NL is closed under coordinate compounding. It seems that there are, a priori ontological commitments aside (see

---

[7] With respect to the categorically more general closure principle (7), it might appear that there are violations in the realm of nominals: since compounds like (i) are ill-formed:

    (i) * *I and John*

Nonetheless, there is a well-formed English coordinate compound of the nominals *I* and *John*:

    (ii) *John and I*

Hence the ungrammaticality in question does not falsify coordinate closure for the English category Nominal.

The argument about NL magnitude we have given does not require the full strength of the proposed closure principles but would be compatible with a weaker principle allowing a limited number of special cases where compounds are impossible.

chapter 6), exactly as good grounds for believing the latter as the former.

Principle (8) mentions a set U of constituents but says nothing about its magnitude. Clearly, one obtains a variety of different closure laws by imposing differential magnitude requirements on U, for instance:

(17) a. U has less than k elements (k a positive finite integer).
  b. U has less than $\aleph_0$ elements.
  c. U has less than $\aleph_1$ elements.
  d. U has less than $\aleph_2$ elements.

There are infinitely many possible magnitude restrictions on U, each limiting the collection of possible projection sets for coordinate compounds. If any of these are adopted *instead of* (8), the argument that an NL is not a set will obviously not go through, because at some point in the definitions of sets S_3, S_4, etc., schematized in (15), the resulting coordinate compounds will not be determined to be included in that NL.

More precisely, if one of the denumerably many restrictions in (17a) is chosen, the collection of coordinate compounds is not determined to be more than a finite set, while if (17b) is chosen, it is a countably infinite set. Consequently, it is critical for the conclusion that (8) rather than any element of (17) is the *correct* closure principle for coordinate compounding. In particular, it is critical to justify (8) against (17b).

A strict parallelism holds between the possible magnitude restrictions in (17) and the various size (length) laws for NL sentences discussed in section 3.3. Hence an argument exactly parallel to that in section 3.3 shows that none of the infinite possibilities represented by (17) can be chosen over (8). For (8) shares the crucial formal property of our view about sentence size (length): *it says nothing at all about magnitude.* On the contrary, each principle of (17) shares the key formal property of the length laws considered in section 3.3 by making some specific claim about maximum magnitude. But any such choice leads to a complication, and thus will be rejected by Occam's razor, unless it can be argued that some basic justified ontological or methodological principles proper to linguistics justify the particular boundaries.

Chapter 6 shows that there are no such justified boundaries for linguistics, no methodological or ontological grounds for excluding all objects greater than some fixed size from the realm of linguistic characterization. Occam's razor is then applicable, since it is always simpler not to specify anything about the magnitude of some set than to say something about its size. And this obviously holds for U in (8). Consequently, the logic leading to a rejection of all NL sentence size laws and to conclusion (6) of chapter 3 leads to the rejection of all magnitude laws on the set U and to the maximally general closure principle (8) rather than to some less general closure law with an arbitrary size bound.

There is a slightly different way to frame the justification for (8) as against any element of (17), which again applies exactly to the justification of (6) of chapter 3 as againt any NL size law. One can regard grammars and grammatical theory as concerned with *projecting* from the properties of *attested* NL sentences, the basic data of grammatical investigation, to the maximal lawfully characterized collections of which these attested sentences are accidental examples. One wants, given a sample of English sentences, to characterize the collection of all English sentences, and, given a sample of NL sentences, the collection of NL sentences per se. General scientific principles demand that the projections from the small finite samples to the desired characterizations involve the maximally general laws (principles) projecting the regularities found in observed cases to the collections as wholes. Putting aside the ontological and methodological grounds for limiting projections discussed in chapter 6, one can then never justifiably replace a more general projection by a less general one unless this is factually motivated; in particular, by the excess generality leading to some false entailment, e.g. a false claim about attested examples, some contradiction, etc.

Therefore, there is no basis for not projecting from attested sentences of various lengths to the maximally general view that sentences of any length whatever are possible, unless this yields some false entailment, which has never been shown. Hence our conclusion (6) of chapter 3. Similarly, there is no basis for not projecting from attested coordinate compounds of various lengths to the maximally general view, represented by (8), that coordinate compounds of any length whatever are possible, unless this yields some false entailment, which again has never been shown. Hence it follows that there is no basis for replacing (8) by any less general principle limiting the magnitude of the set U.

Obviously, the conclusion which (8) determines, that NLs are megacollections, is itself no basis whatever for rejecting this principle, any more than the conclusion which Halmos' Axiom of Powers determines, that the collection of all sets is a megacollection, is a ground for rejecting that axiom. Essentially, principle (8) says that it makes no more sense to think that structures otherwise having the structural (linguistic) properties of coordinate compounds nonetheless fail to be coordinate compounds if they have more than some fixed number of conjuncts than it does to think that aggregates fail to be sets if they have more than some fixed number of elements. That is, it is as arbitrary to claim that some structures have too many conjuncts to be proper coordinate compound sentences as it is to claim that some aggregates have too many elements to be (power) sets.

To sum up, (8), the principle of closure under coordinate compounding, plays an absolutely crucial role in the argument that NLs are megacollections. More precisely, it is the critical assumption guaranteeing that NLs are models of a system of mathematical objects for which all the mathematical assumptions underlying the proof of the NL Vastness Theorem hold.

We have stressed the similarity between the methodological justification for principle (8) and that for principle (6) of chapter 3. Indeed, they are entirely parallel. Conclusion (6) of chapter 3 says there are no size bounds on NL sentences in general, while (8) says, inter alia, that there are no size limits on the number of conjuncts which can form a proper coordinate compound sentence. Both principles are justified by the same general logic. See chapter 6 for further discussion.

However, while these two principles can be provided with parallel methodological justifications in terms of maximally simple and general projections from attested sentences, it does not follow and is not true that the two principles play logically parallel and independent roles in a grammatical theory. In fact, they are not independent since the absence of a least upper bound on NL sentence length is a consequence of the closure principle. To show this, we will again use the predicate *Length* mentioned in chapter 2. We now take this to be a measure of the number of words in a sentence. We also make use of the self-evident fact that the length of any coordinate projection is not less than the cardinality of its projection set. This is only to say that each member of a projection set T contributes at least one word to the coordinate projection of T.

(18)   The *No Upper Bound Theorem*
        THEOREM: Let L be the collection of all sentences of some NL. Then:

   $(\forall k)(\text{Cardinal}(k) \rightarrow$

$$(\exists X)(X \in L \wedge \text{Length}(x) > k))$$
        Proof:
   a. Assume to the contrary that j is a cardinal such that:

$$(\forall X)(X \in L \rightarrow \text{Length}(X) < j).$$

   b. Every proper subset of L then has a cardinality $<j$. For the closure axiom (8) determines that every such subset is the projection set of some coordinate projection which is a sentence of L. And, as we have seen, the length of any coordinate projection is at least that of the cardinality of its projection set. Hence if some $C \subset L$ had $>j$ members, some $Z \in L$ would have a length $>j$, namely, for a Z equal to a coordinate projection of C.

   c. We now show that if every proper subset of L has a cardinality $<j$, the maximal cardinality of L is j. There are two cases, since L is either finite or not finite.

      (i)   Case A. L is finite. Consider one member, M, of the set of *biggest* proper subsets of L. M will have one less member than L. Since M has, from b., a cardinality $<j$, the maximum cardinality of L is j.

      (ii) Case B. L is transfinite. It follows from set theory that there is a one-to-one correspondence between L and some proper subset of L, call it D. Since, from b., D has a cardinality $<j$, so does L.

> d. It follows from c. that L is a set with $\leqslant j$ members, contradicting the NL Vastness Theorem. Hence a. is false.

The fact that the absence of a size law for NL sentences follows from the closure principle provides further justification of a logically independent kind for the non-existence of a size law. Earlier, we argued that eliminating size laws provided the simplest and most general theory and the only one which did not falsely exclude infinitely many well-formed sentences from each NL. The No Upper Bound Theorem shows, in addition, that imposing any size law, finite or transfinite, on NL sentence length, would be incompatible with the simple and powerful principle governing coordinate compounding. That is, closure under coordinate compounding guarantees that there are NL sentences whose size is greater than any given cardinal, finite or transfinite; more specifically, this principle immediately determines for each proper subset of sentences in an NL of some cardinality the existence of a sentence with a length of at least that cardinality.

From this point of view, the purpose of our argument against size laws in chapter 3 should now be clarified. The absence of size laws does not figure as a premiss in the NL Vastness Theorem, so the argumentation of chapter 3 was not concerned with supporting non-mathematical premises of that theorem. Rather, chapter 3 was intended to eliminate an a priori set of assumptions which precluded the result we wished to demonstrate and to show that there was no factual or logical basis for principles which turn out to be logically inconsistent with that result. Put differently, chapter 3 shows that (i) there is no support for any size law, each of which is inconsistent with the NL Vastness Theorem and hence each of which would falsify the coordinate closure principle and (ii) there is support for the view that there is no size law for NL sentences.

The consequence that NLs are megacollections rather than recursively enumerable sets cannot be rationally avoided by a decision to adopt the finiteness limitation on sentence size or its analogue for the number of conjuncts even in the absence of substantively or logically motivated bases for such conditions. We are rejecting an argument which might go something like (19).

(19)   The finiteness limitations are justified just because they
        subsume NLs within the realm of recursively enu-
        merable sets and Turing machine grammars, a math-
        ematically well-understood domain about which a
        rich, useful body of knowledge has been accumu-
        lated.

The fallacy in such a defense of size law (2) of chapter 3 or of a
closure principle like (17b) has already in effect been uncovered by
Chomsky several times in different contexts. First, consider
Chomsky (1957: 23):

We might arbitrarily decree that such processes of sentence
formation in English as those we are discussing cannot be
carried out more than n times, for some fixed n. This would
of course make English a finite state language, as, for
example, would a limitation of English sentences to length of
less than a million words. *Such arbitrary limitations serve no
useful purpose, however.* (our emphasis)

While Chomsky's comment about 'fixed n' was intended only to
cover finite instantiations of n, the force of the remarks clearly
carried over to his own choice of size law (2) of chapter 3 and all
others as well, since these are nothing but instances where n varies
over transfinite cardinals. The same point applies to (17b).
    Again, criticizing a certain argument which need not concern
us, Chomsky (1977a: 174) rightly observed:

In the first place, he is overlooking the fact that we have
certain antecedently clear cases of language as distinct from
maze running, basket weaving, topological orientation,
recognition of faces or melodies, use of maps, and so on. We
cannot arbitrarily decide that 'language' is whatever meets
some canons we propose. Thus we cannot simply stipulate
that rules are structure-independent, ...

Since NLs are independently given, they are not subject to arbitrary decisions about sentence length or any other property. Just
as one cannot simply decide that rules are (or are not) structure-

dependent, one cannot just decide that sentences are (or are not) all finite, or that the number of conjuncts in a coordinate compound is always finite. In both cases, arguments based on the nature of the attested part of the subject matter are required. Consequently, one can no more decide that each sentence is finite in length than one can decide that each is less than one thousand morphemes in length or that each grammar is a finite state system. Unfortunately for linguistics, the sentence finiteness decision has been arbitrarily made and maintained for nearly thirty years. But this past mistake contains no justification for its continuation.

4.4   Simpler proofs of the NL Vastness Theorem

Having given a relatively complicated demonstration of the NL Vastness Theorem, one can consider whether there are simpler proofs. Consider, for example, a construction like (20), in which there is no bound on the number of repetitions:

(20)   a.   Jack is very tall.
            b.   Jack is very very tall.
            c.   Jack is very very ... very$_k$ tall.

In the absence of a least upper bound on constituent size, not only are there $\aleph_0$ sentences of the form in (20), with one distinct string for each instantiation of k as a finite cardinal, there is also one distinct string of the form in (20) of each distinct transfinite length. But that means that there are as many sentences of the form in (20) as there are transfinite cardinals, which is to say a megacollection (Eisenberg (1971: 310)).

Or, again, consider embedded restrictive relative clauses as in:

(21)   a.   I saw someone who saw a nurse who saw a man.
       b.   I saw someone who saw a nurse who saw a man who saw a nurse.
       c.   I saw someone who saw a nurse who saw a man who saw a nurse who saw a man.
       d.   I saw someone who saw a nurse who saw a man ... who saw a nurse who saw a man$_k$.

The structure in (21) is one of the form *I saw someone* followed by *k* instances of the structure *who saw a nurse who saw a man*. For finite *k*, this characterizes a countably infinite set of such structures. But if there is no upper bound, finite or transfinite, on *k*, it follows that there is one such structure for each cardinal number, hence, again, a megacollection of such sentences.

It is important to avoid one particular confusion with respect to arguments like those just given. Focus on (20). The assumption that there is no *finite* upper bound on the number of repetitions is equivalent to the view that one can take any example of the form in (20), add on one more instance of *very* and the result is an English sentence. But of course the assumption that there is no upper bound at all on repetitions, finite or transfinite, is *not* characterizable in this way, for the same interpretation is not possible for the transfinite cases. Even limiting attention to the shortest transfinite string of *very*'s, that with $\aleph_0$ repetitions, there is no way to obtain this string by any operation which yields finite objects when applied to finite objects. This is really to say no more than that $\aleph_0$ is an inaccessible cardinal number (see Kuratowski and Mostowski (1976: 348)), that is, one with no immediate predecessor. Therefore, the assumption that there are transfinite sentences, in particular, transfinite repetitions of the form in (20), (21), etc., is not at all equivalent to the claim that transfinite structures can actually be formed out of smaller structures in some specifiable way. To assume this would, in effect, be to smuggle in the (false) view that the collection of sentences is constructable, that is, forms a recursively enumerable, hence countable set of finite structures. It should be clear that arguments analogous to those based on (20) and (21) can be constructed for any construction which would be regarded as recursive in generative grammatical terms. The non-set (megacollection) character of NLs then apparently manifests in many areas, not simply in the domain of coordination.

While we see no objections to arguments like those based on (20) and (21), such arguments differ significantly from the proof of the NL Vastness Theorem based on closure under coordinate compounding. First, as already indicated, the proof of the latter does not take the non-existence of a bound on sentence length as a premiss but, on the contrary, yields it as a corollary. The proofs we sketched based on (20) and (21) depend, however, entirely on the assumption that there is no least upper bound on sentence size. Second, the proof of the NL Vastness Theorem is based on a principle which is a projection of a truth about all attested sentences into the domain of all sentences, finite and transfinite. There is no analogue of any such principle in our discussion of (20) or (21), nor is it clear that one could be constructed. Because of these differences, it seems clear that at the least, the proof of the megacollection character of NLs based on closure under coordinate compounding is far more fundamental and significant. To reject this proof is not only to reject the idea that there is no bound on sentence length but to insist on complicating a principle needed to predict facts about finite sentences. In this sense, the proof in (16) above rests on positive assumptions which should be deeply embedded in a proper grammatical theory, while the proofs sketched with respect to (20) and (21) rest only on negative factors, namely, the absence of any explicit law limiting sentence size. Put slightly differently, the argument in (16) does not *assume* there are transfinite sentences but displays a principle, the closure principle, based on finite sentences, which *entails* there are transfinite sentences, in fact, transfinite sentences of every cardinality.

5

Implications

5.0   Remarks

Chapters 3 and 4 of this study respectively establish the following two relatively simple substantive points about NLs:

(1)   a.   There is no basis for imposing any size law on NL sentences (see also chapter 6).

   b.   The NL Vastness Theorem; that is, the existence of unbounded coordination subject to the closure principle (8) of chapter 4 entails, via a Cantorian analogy, that the collection of sentences in an NL is (i) bigger than countably infinite, and (ii), in fact, a megacollection.

Moreover, we showed that (1a) is a logical consequence of the closure principle (see the No Upper Bound Theorem), which thus provides a principled reason for the non-existence of NL size laws. Since the argument for (1b) was based exclusively on English data, it is more accurate to say that (1b) follows for an NL manifesting coordination with the essential properties characterized in section 4.1.

However, we know of no NL ever described which has even been *claimed* to lack coordination of, inter alia, clauses. As Dik (1968: 1) puts it:

For a variety of reasons the so-called 'coordinative construction' is of special importance to linguistic theory. In the first place, this type of construction seems to be a universal feature of natural languages. Secondly, not only does its existence seem to be universal, but the way in which it is mani-

fested in each particular language also shows a quite general,
if not universal pattern.

The relevance of this universality for our argument is not removed
by the observation of E. Keenan (personal communication) that
there are NLs in which conjunct clauses have somewhat different
forms than the 'corresponding' clauses occuring as main clauses.
To formulate the argument in such cases, it would merely be
necessary to supplement the notion of coordinate projection with
functions which map independent clauses into the particular forms
they have when appearing as subconjuncts. Since the argument
that NLs are megacollections involves the cardinality of sets, such
differences in form, which fail to affect cardinality, will be inessential. Further, the argument in chapter 3 is quite independent of
any facts about English. Consequently, we hypothesize that both
(1a, b) are proper universal truths about NLs.

5.1 Basic consequences

An initial group of implications from (1) are negative. It can be
used, as earlier discerned facts about the nature of NLs have been,
to falsify proposed grammatical theories on the grounds that their
expressive power is too weak. Just as certain facts about NLs were
taken to show that finite state grammars (Chomsky (1957)),
context-free grammars,[1] etc., are too weak, the fact that NLs are
megacollections shows that any conception of grammars under
which they are Turing machines is inadequate. Put differently, (1b)
entails that any theory which claims NLs are recursively enumerable sets is false. We formulate this consequence explicitly as a
theorem referred to as the *NL Non-constructivity Theorem*.

(2)   THEOREM: No NL has any constructive (= proof-
        theoretic, generative or Turing machine) grammar.
        Proof:
        a. Let L be an NL and let G be a constructive
            grammar.

---

[1] Pullum and Gazdar (1982) show, however, that no previous argument for the
inability of CF grammars to weakly generate NLs really stands up.

b. G specifies exactly some collection, call it C(G). From the definition of constructive systems, G recursively enumerates C(G), which is hence a countably infinite or finite set.
c. the NL Vastness Theorem shows that L is a mega-collection.
d. Hence (see Eisenberg (1971: 304)), L has more elements than C(G) and, consequently, C(G) ≠ L.
e. Therefore, G is not a grammar of L.

Since G and L in (2) were arbitrarily chosen, it has been shown that *no* constructive system is a correct grammar of *any* NL.[2]

Although the NL Non-constructivity Theorem is straightforward, its consequences are both extraordinarily broad and deep. For, as Chomsky (1957: 34) correctly observed: 'The strongest possible proof of the inadequacy of a linguistic theory is to show that it literally cannot apply to some natural language.' In Chomsky's terms then, the NL Non-constructivity Theorem shows that every variant of every view taking NL grammars to be constructive devices is a *false* theory of NLs. This means that every logically possible variant (not only those *so far* described) of all the frameworks in (3) are false:

(3) Frameworks Falsified as Theories of NLs by the NL Non-constructivity Theorem:
Finite Grammar (Hockett (1968))
Finite State Grammar (Reich (1969))

---

[2] The full generalization depends of course on the view that (1) holds for all NLs.
Consequence (2) should be compared with the constantly repeated claim that unconstrained transformational grammars (= Turing machines) are in general too *strong*, allow too huge a superset of NLs to be of any interest, e.g. Chomsky and Lasnik (1977: 425–6): 'Early work in pursuit of descriptive adequacy led to an extremely rich theory of TG ... If this judgement is correct, then the problem we face is to restrict the options that are available in this narrower, but *still overly permissive framework*, ...' (our emphasis). Similarly, Bach (1974: 158) remarks: 'A fairly large literature on the formal properties of transformational grammars of various sorts has shown that the theory is much too powerful.' The fact that transformational grammars, like all other Turing-machine subtypes, are too weak along the size parameter to characterize NLs does not, however, preclude their having *excessive* descriptive power along other dimensions.

Phrase Structure Grammar (Harmon (1963); Gazdar (1981a, 1982))

Lexical/Functional Grammar (Bresnan (1980, 1982))

Realistic Grammar (Brame (1979))

Stratificational Grammar (Lamb (1966); Lockwood (1972))

Tagmemics (Longacre (1964))

Montague Grammar (Partee (1975, 1976); Dowty (1978, 1982))

Natural Generative Grammar (Bartsch and Vennemann (1972))

Semantically-Based Grammar (Chafe (1970a, 1970b))

Functional Grammar (Dik (1978, 1980))

Daughter Dependency Grammar (Hudson (1976); Schachter (1978))

Phrasal Core Grammar (Keenan (1980a, 1980b))

Transformational Grammar (Chomsky (1957, 1965, 1977b, 1981a, 1982))

Corepresentational Grammar (Kac (1980))

Relationally-Based Grammar (Johnson (1979))

Dependency Grammar (Hays (1964))

Categorial Grammar (Lambek (1961))

Cognitive Grammar (Lakoff and Thompson (1975))

Meaning-Text Models (Mel'čuk (1981))

The Abstract System (Harris (1968))

Configurational Grammar (Koster (1981))

Neostructural Grammar (Langendoen (1982))

Augmented Transition Networks (Woods (1970))

String Adjunct Grammar (Joshi, Kosaraju and Yamada (1972))

Equational Grammar (Sanders (1972))

Systemic Grammar (Hudson (1971))

Any *constructive* system distinct from all of the preceding frameworks.

The NL Non-constructivity Theorem actually follows from a conclusion *infinitely weaker* than the NL Vastness Theorem, namely, just from the fact that NLs are at least of the magnitude of the continuum, which suffices to justify conclusion (2d) with no reference to megacollections. Hence the stage of the analogy in section 4.2 involving just the set there called S_1 already suffices to falsify all views limiting grammars to the characterization of recursively enumerable sets. This means the conclusion follows from consideration of sentences of no greater than denumerably infinite length. In fact, the existence of a single denumerably infinite sentence suffices to show that an NL has no constructive grammar.

The NL Non-constructivity Theorem is unaffected by questions of metagrammars and rule schemata. Allowing a grammar to be an infinite set of finite proof-theoretic rules characterized by a finite metagrammar does not permit the (infinite) grammar to characterize anything other than a recursively enumerable set; see Langendoen (1976).

Of course, the NL Non-constructivity Theorem does not show that *everything* about the frameworks in (3) is incorrect. Considering only the entailments of (2) itself, it is logically possible to preserve anything in these frameworks which could be made compatible with the megacollection character of NLs. In almost every case, it would be possible to preserve the various conceptions of the nature of NL sentences. It is the notion of grammar/grammatical rule inherent to these frameworks which is incorrect. But, as Chomsky (1972b: 78) stressed: 'Of course, all would agree that the fundamental problem of linguistic theory is to determine what kinds of rules ... exist.'

The NL Non-constructivity Theorem states that no NL has a constructive grammar. It might be wondered just to what extent the NL Vastness Theorem is incompatible with constructivity. In particular, given the syntactic nature of the data on which the NL Vastness Theorem is based, one might assume that the result was compatible, for example, with either or both constructive phonology and/or (interpretive) semantics. But this is not the case. A grammar capable of characterizing transfinite sentences cannot contain constructive phonological or semantic components.

To show this, we will focus on phonology. It has been assumed in generative work that each NL grammar involves a phonological component (PC) consisting of a finite set of rules, interpreted as a Turing machine. More precisely, the PC has been interpreted as a transducer, taking as inputs elements of a recursively enumerable set of trees (surface structures) and associating with each an object (string) called a phonetic representation.

Under the constructive (Turing machine) interpretation of the PC, each rule is an operation, and of each phonetic representation has a finite derivation from its underlying surface structure via a finite number of finite applications of the phonological rules. In different terms, each phonetic representation has a finite 'proof' (= sequence of finite lines), each formed from the preceding by a finite number of rule applications. The phonological rules thus play the role of rules of inference in genuine proof systems.

But NLs contain transfinite sentences. Pick one of the shortest of such sentences, one with a denumerable length. And consider the interaction of such a sentence with the PC as traditionally characterized. For concreteness, take German word-final devoicing, representable schematically via a rule good enough for current purposes as:

(4)   Stop ———→ -Voice/__#

Clearly, the informal intention is that such rules minimally have the consequence that *every* word final stop in *every* German word in *every* German sentence is voiceless. This intended consequence will, moreover, be a real consequence under the Turing machine interpretation for every finite German sentence, barring other (later ordered) rules etc. which (re)voice etc., matters which we can ignore.

Consider then a denumerably long transfinite German sentence and, moreover, one with infinitely many underlying voiced word-final stops. Clearly there will be such, since no principle limits the number of words in a German sentence which can have underlyingly voiced word-final stops. Evidently though, no Turing machine interpretation of rule (4) can provide the intended result for such sentences, that is, one in which *every* underlying word-final voiced stop is devoiced. For, after any finite number of applications of (4) to a structure containing infinitely many word-final voiced stops, there would remain infinitely many which would *not* have been devoiced. Thus a constructive phonology of the sort assumed in generative phonology cannot work for transfinite sentences and consequently is in general inadequate.

To avoid this consequence, it will not do just to abandon the intended consequence of rules like (4) for transfinite sentences.

That is, one could not rationally claim that in transfinite sentences (infinitely) many word-final stops in German need *not* be voiceless. This would be as arbitrary and unjustified as the parallel claim for extremely long finite sentences, say those with ten to the thousandth power words. The purpose of grammatical rules is to project from the few, relatively short theoretically accidental examples of an NL one can manage to examine to the maximally general laws governing the entire collection of sentences. These projections should, on general grounds, be the strongest claims compatible with known facts. Therefore, if one finds word-final devoicing in all *attested* sentences, the maximally general projection is that it holds in all sentences, not only in all shorter than some arbitrarily fixed cardinal.

It follows that there is no possibility of having e.g. a non-constructive syntax to satisfy the NL Non-constructivity Theorem combined with a constructive phonology. Transfinite sentences are incompatible with proof-theoretic phonologies as well. Moreover, it is easy to see that the logic applied to rule (4) would equally apply to any attempt at proof-theoretic *semantic* rules. There can then be no viable Turing machine (computable function) semantic component either. In short, the consequences for the nature of NL grammars derivable from the argument to the NL Non-constructivity Theorem are total. It is not just the generative grammar view of syntax which collapses, but also that of phonology and semantics.

The implications of the NL-Non-constructivity Theorem can be summed up as follows. Since the ideas of generative grammar became dominant in the late 1950s, linguistics has in general assumed that the task of grammatical theory involves answering the question: What is the right form of *generative* grammar for NLs? The many disputes which have divided linguists over the past quarter century are then reducible by and large to disputes over claims about 'right form'. Some linguists have believed that NL grammars contain transformational rules; others have denied this. Some linguists have believed that transformational rules are parochially ordered; others have denied this. Some linguists have believed that there are interpretive semantic rules; others have denied this. And so on. Underlying all such disputes has been the assumption that it is possible through appeal to some combination of proof-theoretical devices to construct *some* generative grammar for each NL. But this assumption is entirely falsified by the NL Non-constructivity Theorem.

A historical parallel might help clarify the implications of this theorem. In the early twentieth century, under the influence of the great mathematician David Hilbert, it was widely assumed that it would be possible to characterize the notion 'mathematical truth' in terms of provability or theoremhood. That is, Hilbert assumed, as the essence of a philosophy of mathematics called formalism, that it would be possible to find a finite set of axioms from which all of the truths of mathematics would follow as theorems, where, moreover, the notion 'follow' could be reduced to a limited number of simple, mechanical, finite principles of inference. The idea was that via a formalization of mathematics it would be possible to demonstrate that it was free of contradictions, that is, that none of the paradoxes would arise; see Fraenkel, Bar-Hillel and Levy (1973: 275–80), Kleene (1952: 53–9), Kreisel (1964). The problem viewed from the vantage point of Hilbert's program was essentially one of formalization: to reduce mathematics to finite manipulations of finite strings of symbols. The goal was thus to find the right set of axioms and the right characterization of the principles of inference.

Given any proposed axiomatization, it would have been possible to dispute its tenability by quarreling with the axioms or with the characterization of the principles of inference, all while remaining internal to the assumptions of Hilbert's formalism. In the same way, one can quarrel with any version of the generative philosophy of linguistics introduced by Chomsky by quarreling with the choice of generative grammatical theory, with the choice of particular grammatical rules for some NL, etc., all while remaining internal to that philosophy.

However, in 1931 Kurt Gödel proved theorems which in effect completely undermined Hilbert's formalist philosophy. According to Gödel's results, there could not in principle be any consistent finite set of axioms from which even the full set of truths about arithmetic followed as theorems. Arithmetical truth, hence, more generally mathematical truth, turned out to be in principle a far richer and more extensive notion than the notion of theorem finitely provable from some set of axioms. Gödel's theorems thus undermined not specific assumptions internal to Hilbert's formalism, but the whole program itself, which was unrealizable due to the nature of mathematical truth. No tinkering with the axioms or principles of inference could ever reach Hilbert's goal, which is unachievable, because its most basic assumptions are false.

We claim that the NL Non-constructivity Theorem bears roughly the same relation to Chomsky's generative philosophy as Gödel's incompleteness theorems do to Hilbert's formalist philosophy. Just as no tinkering with the devices of Hilbert's program could ever yield a consistent finite axiomatization of all arithmetical truth, no tinkering with the devices of generative linguistics can ever yield a grammar of an NL. The NL Non-constructivity Theorem shows that the whole underlying generative philosophy is wrong; like Hilbert's program, the generative program seeks to accomplish the impossible. Whereas Hilbert's program misconstrued the nature of mathematical truth, the generative program misconstrues the nature of NL sentences, unjustifiably ignoring transfinite sentences. This has led generative linguistics to misconstrue the nature of NL grammars, as made explicit by the NL Non-conductivity Theorem.

We have drawn a parallelism between the undermining of Hilbert's program by Gödel's incompleteness theorems and the undermining of the generative program by the NL Non-constructivity Theorem. This parallelism is not in the least weakened by the essential mathematical triviality of the latter theorem in comparison with the former. The parallelism is based not on the formal character of the proofs but on the way they show the unrealizability of certain intellectual programs, moreover, intellectual programs which share a high degree of institutionalization, public support and association with renowned figures. Just as Gödel's results showed that a viable mathematics could not be built on a basis of formalism, the results in chapter 4 show that a viable grammatical study cannot be erected on the basis of the generative philosophy. It is perhaps worth adding, however, that there is a certain formal parallelism between the results. The incompleteness results show in effect (see Kleene (1952: especially chapter 11); Fraenkel, Bar-Hillel and Levy (1973: 309)) that the collection of truths of elementary number theory do not form a recursively enumerable set; the results in chapter 4 show that the collection of sentences of an NL do not form a set, hence, a fortiori, not a recursively enumerable set. Thus, the formalist philosophy, which assumed that every mathematical truth corresponds to some finitist proof in a single consistent system, and the generative philosophy, which assumes that every sentence in each NL corresponds to some finite proof-theoretic derivation, share underlying similarities of a formal character. It seems fair to say then that both philosophies incorporate an overly simple view of their domains, viewing them incorrectly as recursively enumerable sets.

There is another way to characterize the consequences summed up in (1) and in the NL Non-constructivity Theorem. The false finiteness limitation on sentence size determined the claim that NLs fall somewhere in the domain of objects characterizable by what one might call *theoretical computer science*. Their grammars would be some sort of Turing machine, their sentence aggregates recursively enumerable sets. Since NLs are subject to no size law, they do not lie within this limited class of mathematical objects. While this conclusion may, for various socio-historical reasons, be displeasing to some, it involves no unsurmountable theoretical or methodological difficulties. Logic and the foundations of mathematics faced similar problems at the beginning of this century but did not cease to thrive; quite the contrary. Hence the results in (1) and (2) are not at all to be seen as negative or unhappy consequences for grammatical study. They can be interpreted quite positively, as showing that NLs have a grandeur not previously recognized.

To our knowledge, the one extant view of grammar and grammatical rule which survives the NL Non-constructivity Theorem is the proposal in Johnson and Postal (1980) and Postal (1982). Even this framework does not emerge completely unscathed. The reason this approach to grammars can be kept consistent with (1) is that the conception of NL sentence finiteness, which was arbitrarily and wrongly associated with it, was peripherally imposed, as noted in footnote 1 of chapter 2 and footnote 6 of chapter 3, as a condition on sentences.[3] The sentence finiteness assumption was,

---

[3] Finiteness enters into the characterization of sentence in Johnson and Postal (1980) in another more basic way. Pair networks there are based on a set of non-terminal nodes, identified with the set of integers greater than 4. This allows only a denumerable set of non-terminal nodes to form any sentence. There would not be enough of them to form most transfinite sentences. This inconsistency between the formulation in Johnson and Postal (1980) and the conclusion that NLs are megacollections can be eliminated by drawing non-terminal nodes from

in this framework, *completely independent of the nature of grammars*. Unlike proof-theoretic approaches, nothing inherent in the non-constructive notion of rule/grammar in this work is limited to finite sentences. Consequently, when the arbitrary limitation to finite sentences is eliminated, the conception of grammar does not collapse, as must all formulations taking grammars to be proof-theoretic.

5.2   Non-constructive grammars

Nonetheless, (1) requires minor changes in the formulation of non-constructive grammars (NCG) given in Johnson and Postal (1980) and Postal (1982). Simplifying initially, NCG claimed that the collection of sentences of an arbitrary NL, called a *corpus*, was specified as follows. Grammatical theory provided a definition of 'Sentence', analyzed as the notion Pair Network. Since it was subjected to a transfinite size law analogous to (2) of chapter 3, this definition specified a countably infinite superset of pair networks of which all NLs were said to be subsets.

NCG claimed in addition that grammatical theory contains a set of *sentence laws*. These determine via satisfaction a subset of the set of all pair networks. This subset was called *Universal Sentence* (US) in Postal (1982). US is the subset of all pair networks obeying all sentence laws; equivalently, US is the subset of all pair networks satisfying the single statement which is the logical conjunction of all the sentence laws. Put differently, US is the subcollection of all pair networks for which all of the sentence laws are true. NCG claimed that every NL corpus is a subset of US. To define a particular NL corpus, NCG then assumed that each NL involved a (non-constructive) grammar, consisting of a finite set of *statements*, formulae to which truth values can be assigned (in fact, each was assumed to be conditional). The set of these statements picked out a subset of US via satisfaction in exactly the way that

---

the full hierarchy of transfinite ones. This is analogous to a procedure in infinitary logic, as specified, for example in Chang (1968: 36): 'In order to discuss the extensions of $L_{\lambda\kappa}$ of L, we first specify that there shall be a supply of variables V_ξ one for each ordinal ξ.' Note that the 'supply' in question is a megacollection, since the collection of ordinals is (Eisenberg (1971: 291)).

the set of sentence laws picked out a subset of all pair networks. Hence a particular NL corpus was essentially that subset of US satisfying all the statements forming the grammar of that NL.

The concept of grammar just described is close to the notion of condition in section 1.1. The similarlity is made clearer when it is noted that the set of all individual rules, conceived as statements, is equivalent to some single statement consisting of their logical conjunction. In contrast to the constructive, proof-theoretic approaches falsified by the NL Non-constructivity Theorem, NCG can be considered model-theoretic. The 'function' of rules is not given by interpreting them as operations defined on their syntax, as the rules of inference of a logical or mathematical system, but rather by taking them as statements and determining the objects for which they are true or false. NCG hence has the virtue of largely reducing the principles of interpretation for grammars to standard, basic devices of logic and set-theory.

Our account of NCG so far has ignored an important distinction made in Johnson and Postal (1980), one distinguishing sentence laws and grammatical rules which quantify exclusively over individual sentences and their parts and laws and rules which quantify also over collections of sentences. Johnson and Postal (1980: chapter 14) observed that there are grammatically significant regularities about NLs which are not reducible to statements about individual sentences. Thus, to qualify as an NL, it does not suffice to be a subcollection of US. For instance, the single structure:

(5)   The king loves to hunt

is an English sentence, hence a bona fide subcollection of US, hence satisfies the definition of 'Sentence' and obeys all sentence laws. Yet clearly (5) should not be characterized as an NL. One concludes that there are conditions on NL-hood which refer not only to sentences but to overall collections of sentences. To the extent that these conditions are universals, they were referred to in Johnson and Postal (1980) as *corpus laws*; to the extent that they were NL-specific, they were referred to as *corpus rules*.

The central argument of the current study has been based on a condition having the status of a corpus law, namely, the principle of closure under coordinate compounding of chapter 4. This principle says nothing about the nature of individual sentences but imposes a completeness condition on the collections of sentences capable of being NLs. It precludes, for example, the possibility of an NL otherwise like English in which there is an upper bound, say eight, or eighty, or eight hundred on the maximum number of conjuncts in a conjoined clause. Such a collection would contain only English sentences and thus each of its elements would obey all sentence laws. It can then only be excluded from the realm of NLs by laws quantifying over collections of sentences. The need for a principle precluding finite limits on coordination was noted in Johnson and Postal (1980: 681), but no principle was proposed. Moreover, it is clear in current terms not only that there is no finite least upper bound on the degree of coordinate branching, but no least upper bound at all. It is plausible that the principle referred to by Katz (1978, 1981) as effability (see section 3) would also turn out to be formally represented as a corpus law.

The claim of Johnson and Postal (1980) that each NL corpus is a *subset* of the *set* US requires only a completely trivial reformulation to remain consistent with the result of chapter 4 that NLs are not sets but megacollections. We simply adjust the terminology, recognize that US is a megacollection and thus that each NL corpus is a subcollection of that megacollection. Since subcollecting, like subsetting, does not involve the membership relation, none of the paradoxes or contradictions of set-theory can arise in this way. That is, there is no set-theoretical difficulty in allowing one megacollection to be a subcollection of another. Hence the inclusion claim of Johnson and Postal (1980) is rendered consistent with chapter 4 simply by the terminological change yielding the new claim that every NL corpus is a subcollection of the megacollection US. This assumes, of course, that the arbitrary size law originally part of the definition of 'Sentence' in Johnson and Postal (1980) is eliminated and that the collection of non-terminal nodes is expanded from integers to cardinal (or possibly, ordinal) numbers in general.

However, the formulation in Johnson and Postal (1980) of the relation between individual NL corpora and the realm of all NL corpora, necessary to impose corpus laws on the former, cannot survive in the same way. For inessential reasons, that relation was formulated in terms of membership. It was claimed that grammatical theory specified a set of corpora, each a subset of US and each satisfying all corpus laws. Each NL was then a *member* of this set. Given the NL Vastness Theorem, this approach does not work, and cannot be reformulated in anything like the analogous way. One simply cannot talk about a collection of all NL corpora. Since each NL corpus is a megacollection, there simply is no such collection, under pain of contradiction.

The necessity then arises of formulating a new account of corpora which both imposes all corpus laws and yet makes no appeal to membership. One can approach this task as follows. Grammatical theory is concerned with specifying the nature of NLs; a priori, one might have assumed this could be done by specifying the membership of a collection, or even set, of NLs. But the theorem showing that NLs are megacollections shows there is no such collection. The realm of all NLs is thus parallel to the realm of all collections, which also forms no collection. Nonetheless, set-theories are possible ... theories which give necessary and sufficient conditions for anything to be a collection/set. In the same way, grammatical theories are possible, theories which state the necessary and sufficient conditions for being an NL. We can assume that such a theory takes the form of a definition of 'NL', into which are built the analogues of the axioms of a set-theory.[4]

For reasons already cited, we assume the existence of a set of corpus laws, one of which is some form of principle (8) of chapter 4. Let us refer to the single statement consisting of the logical conjunction of all corpus laws as COLA. Then we might initially specify the nature of NLs as follows:

$$
\begin{aligned}
(6) \qquad (\forall X)(NL(X) &\leftrightarrow X \subseteq US \wedge COLA(X) \\
&\wedge (\exists Y)(Grammar(Y) \wedge Y \\
&= \{SR_i, CR_j\} \wedge CR_j(X) \\
&\wedge ((\forall z)(z \in X \rightarrow SR_i(z)))))
\end{aligned}
$$

This is to be interpreted as follows. Here X ranges over collections of sentences. The defining expression for 'NL(X)' has three con-

---

[4] Proposal of a definition like (6) yields a disanalogy between grammatical theory and set-theories. This is due to the fact that the notion of a collection is so fundamental that it cannot be defined, even when membership is taken as primitive (note that the null collection has no members). Thus Gödel's (1964: 262) remark: 'The operation "set of x's" (where the variable "x" ranges over some given kind of objects) cannot be defined satisfactorily (at least not in the present state of knowledge), ...' Consequently, 'collection' is a primitive, while 'NL' turns out, it is claimed, to be definable.

juncts. The first says that to be an NL, X must be a subcollection of the collection US, which is, recall, the collection of all objects satisfying the definition of 'Sentence' and also satisfying all sentence laws. Hence the first conjunct of the defining expression simply says that an NL is a collection of sentences each of which satisfies all sentence laws. The second conjunct requires in addition that X itself satisfy all the corpus laws, and hence, in particular, given chapter 4 above, that it be a collection closed under coordinate compounding, hence having coordinate structures of every length, finite and transfinite.

The third conjunct of the defining expression in (6) is designed to relate NLs to grammars. This conjunct need not necessarily beg the question of whether there are NLs without finite grammars, or even without grammars at all. This will not really be excluded if, for example, the definition of 'Grammar', which we have of course not given, allows the null string as a grammar and allows transfinite as well as finite grammars.[5] Moreover, the formulation does not beg the question of whether the same NL can have distinct grammars.[6] Nonetheless, for the interesting cases, G will be non-null and finite. The assumption is that just as grammatical laws are divided into statements quantifying over sentences and those also quantifying over collections of sentences, so are individual grammar statements (see Johnson and Postal (1980) for discussion). From this point of view, each grammar is a pair, one of whose members is a collection of sentence rules, the other of which is a collection of corpus rules. Equivalently, grammars can be thought of as pairs whose members are a single logical conjunction of sentence rules and a single logical conjunction of corpus rules. Assume that 'SR_i' is some proper logical conjunction of sentence rules, that is, a logical conjunction of statements quantifying only over sentences and their parts, while 'CR_j' is some proper logical conjunction of corpus rules, that is, rules quantifying over collections of sentences. By 'proper' here we mean in

---

[5] While one certainly wants each attested (in fact, attestable) NL to have at least one *finite* non-constructive grammar, there is nothing in principle wrong with a theory which also characterizes infinite grammars. Such grammars are, however, not even of formal interest unless they can in some sense be shown to be at least one order of magnitude smaller than their extensions.

[6] There is no reason to think that grammars of NLs are unique, nor any reason to be troubled by the existence of intensionally distinct grammars which specify the same extension. This does, however, raise questions about language learning.

accord with whatever constraints on such rules a correct grammatical theory imposes. Then the third conjunct in the defining expression of (6) says that X must also satisfy CR_j and that each member of X must satisfy SR_i. In these terms then, an NL is a subcollection of US satisfying all corpus laws and satisfying the corpus rule of its grammar and which is such that each of its members satisfies the sentence rule of its grammar.

A key feature of (6), which is of course merely a sketch, is that the notion of *membership*, which can yield the set-theoretical paradoxes, enters only at a single point. In (6), membership only relates individual sentences to collections, and thus is perfectly harmless. At no point are NLs themselves, which are megacollections, allowed to be members of anything. That is, (6) involves no reference to a collection of NLs. Hence, (6) reconstructs all of the essential ideas of the non-constructive approach to grammar in Johnson and Postal (1980) and yet maintains consistency with the result of chapter 4, that is, with the NL Vastness Theorem.

We have claimed from chapter 1 on that allowing megacollections to be members yields the basic set-theoretical paradoxes. Chapter 4 showed that NLs are megacollections, hence apparently too big to be elements of anything. Consequently, even though this is standard and apparently natural, it is as impossible to speak of a grammatical theory as characterizing a set or even a collection of NLs as it is to speak of set-theory as characterizing the set of all sets. Since each NL corpus is a megacollection, there is no collection of NLs.[7] This sort of difficulty, to the extent that the consequence is properly regarded as such, is only a special case of parallel implications in set-theory itself, more precisely, in

[7] Because of this fact, it is not possible to deal with idiolect/dialect questions as in Katz (1981: 9): 'Relative to a solution, Platonism can group idiolects as a dialect and dialects as a language in terms of conditions for set membership over classes of abstract objects (sets of sentences so construed). There is an infinite range of such classes, including English, French, Sanskrit, Engrench (i.e., a class of sentences with English syntactic structure but an anglicized French vocabulary), and infinitely many other languages, living, dead, unborn, conceivable and inconceivable.' Since the collections of sentences forming idiolects or dialects are megacollections, they cannot be members of any collections. Thus NLs cannot be collections of dialects nor dialects collections of idiolects. It is unclear how one should rebuild Katz's account to achieve consistency with this consequence.

any set-theory which recognizes megacollections, as observed by Quine (1963: 321-2) and Fraenkel, Bar-Hillel and Levy (1973: 142). The latter remark with respect to von Neumann:

> His addition of proper classes to the universe of set theory results from his discovery that it is not the existence of certain classes that leads to the antinomies, but rather the assumption of their elementhood, i.e., their being members of other classes; therefore he introduces these classes as proper classes which are not members of classes. This is not a completely satisfactory solution of the problem of the existence of collections as objects, since now, even though proper classes are real objects, collections of proper classes do not exist. The existence of real mathematical objects which cannot be members of even finite classes is a rather peculiar matter ...

Since we claim to have shown that NLs are megacollections, it follows that internal to linguistics there are 'real mathematical objects' of the sort so far not consistently allowed to be members of collections, if one assumes a set-theory something like von Neumann's. Quine (1963: 321-2) considers ways of allowing megacollections to be members of just finite collections, still precluding the paradoxes. This would be sufficient for certain limited linguistic purposes, for instance, it would allow a reconstruction of the notions of dialect and NL in terms of collections of idiolects and collections of dialects respectively, where the members are finite numbers of megacollections (see footnote 7). However, it would still not permit one to speak of a collection of NLs since, as demonstrated in section 6.4, there are non-finitely many NLs.

From this point of view, it is then relevant, as Fraenkel, Bar-Hillel and Levy (1973: 142-6) note, that there are ways of permitting even non-finitely many megacollections to be elements in a set-theory which is consistent if the more standard set-theories are. In one such approach, one recognizes a type of object, call it a hypercollection, which has as members collections, including megacollections. In these terms, there are three types of aggregate entities – hypercollections, collections and sets – such that all sets are collections and all collections are hypercollections. Perhaps the best set-theory for linguistics is one which recognizes hypercollections; it would then be possible to say that a grammatical theory characterizes the hypercollection of all NLs. This matter requires much further study, since there are other approaches which would permit limited membership possibilities for mega-collections without determining paradoxes.

Even without consideration of hypercollections or analogous devices, one can indicate how grammatical theory characterizes all NLs, just as one can indicate how a set-theory not recognizing a collection of all sets characterizes all sets. In both cases, the task involves stating the laws governing the objects in question. For the realm of NLs, anything satisfying these laws is an NL, nothing else is. Even supposing there is not even a collection of all NLs, this is no more a problem than there being, under the same set-theoretical assumptions, no collection of all collections, or collection of all collections of numbers. Moreover, in the case of NLs, it is possible, as developed in Johnson and Postal (1980: chapter 14), and re-expressed in (6), to regard each NL as a subcollection of a universally characterized collection, US. The fact revealed in chapter 4 that this collection is a megacollection need not preclude this interpretation, whereby each NL sentence falls under the extension of a *universal* class of grammatical laws, and is differentiated from sentences in distinct NLs by being under the extension of *non-universal* statements forming an individual grammar which 'foreign' sentences do not satisfy.

Although, hypercollections and analogous devices aside, the fact that NLs are megacollections prevents them from being members of anything, definable subsets of NLs can consistently be taken as members. For example, all and only the *finite* elements of the megacollection of English can unproblematically be said to be a subset of that subset of US consisting of all and only those elements satisfying both the logical conjunction of all sentence laws and the size law (2) of chapter 3. The specified subset is just the set US of Postal (1982). One can form an analogous set of finite sentences for each NL. Nothing then precludes defining the set of all such sets of finite sentences. Moreover, each successive choice of size law from (3) of chapter 3 for some NL defines a successively bigger subset of that NL. And, at each level or layer, one can consistently state that that subset is a subset of the analogous layer of sentences from US. Again, at each level or layer, the set of sentences drawn from each NL can be consistently taken as a member of the set of all sets of sentences of that layer. The layers are obviously analogous to the subsets S_0, S_1, S_2, ... artificially picked out in our discussion in chapter 4. In this way, the idea of

Johnson and Postal (1980) that the corpus of an NL is a *member* of a universally characterized set of NL corpora can in a loose sense be *approximated*. However, there are infinitely many membership relations, one for each choice of transfinite size law, each giving a subset of some NL and a subset of the collection of all NL sentences.

Obviously, we have only specified here the bare outlines of a conception of non-constructive grammars. Clearly, an actual account will have to say substantive things about the nature of the statements forming grammars in the above description, e.g. limiting them in various ways. These matters need not concern us here.

Unlike generative systems, a non-constructive grammar as just described is entirely consistent with (1). Since NLs are subject to no size law, neither the definition of 'Sentence', nor any grammatical law, nor any grammatical rule in any grammar can be a size law. Hence no object can fail to be subsumed within any NL collection *merely because of its size*, transfinite though that might be. This approach represents precisely Katz's claim in (7) of chapter 3 that the property of well-formedness (the property of being in the collection) is independent of size (length) factors. Moreover, in this non-constructive approach, the fact that sentences are free of size bounds emerges 'automatically'; it is the direct consequence of *saying nothing whatever about sentence size*. Hence the current sketch of a non-constructive approach should clarify the earlier argument that adding any size law would complicate grammatical theory or individual grammars. For such a law would either be (i) an extra definitional component of the definition of 'Sentence', complicating that definition, or (ii) an extra law listed in grammatical theory serving to define US, hence complicating that set of laws, or else (iii) an extra grammatical rule, which is not part of grammatical theory per se (that is, not part of (6)) but which must either be listed or represented as part of individual grammars, uselessly complicating any grammar containing it.

The major positive implication of (1) is then, in our view, that NL grammars have roughly the non-constructive form just sketched.[8] This has various novel consequences, some described in

[8] Since NL grammars cannot be constructive, various historical suggestions (Langendoen (1964); Chomsky (1965: 8)) that a precise or scientific linguistics was inevitably delayed until after the development of the ideas of recursive function theory are quite dubious.

Johnson and Postal (1980: chapter 14) and Postal (1982). Specifically, it has such negative consequences as that NL grammars do
not involve base rules, transformations, interpretive rules, stylistic
rules, lexical insertion rules, etc.; in short, none of the parapher-
nalia which have made up the theoretical subject matter of the
generative linguistic literature. Such devices could at best play a
role in the characterization of finite structures and thus cannot in
principle be part of a general characterization of a realm like that
of NLs most of whose members are transfinite. We in effect explicated this consequence earlier when showing why a proof-
theoretic phonology was incompatible with transfinite sentences.
From this viewpoint, it is no accident that such devices have no
analogues in the principles of set-theory.

We have *not* claimed that the NL Vastness Theorem or anything
else determines that it is logically necessary that NL grammars
have the particular non-constructive form sketched here. All we
have stressed is that (i) this is the only *known* conception of NL
grammars not falsified by the determination that NLs are megacollections and (ii) any viable conception must transcend purely
constructive limitations.

It is worth considering one apparent possibility for a form of
grammars different from that sketched here which might seem to
maintain consistency with the NL Vastness Theorem. Recall that
a standard (generative) account of the unbounded degree of
branching possible in coordinate structures is via rule schemata.
These permit a finite specification of the infinite number of phrase
structure rules necessary under the standard interpretation of
phrase structure rules (see footnote 3 of chapter 2). That is, one
rule is necessary for binary branchings, one for ternary branchings, one for quaternary branchings, etc., yielding a countable
infinitude of rules for the countable infinitude of maximally flat
coordinate branchings found in the subcollection of finite NL
sentences.

A standard way of finitely representing such a countably infinite
set of rules is with rule schemata such as (7):

(7) $S\langle a\rangle \rightarrow S\langle b\rangle^n, \quad n > 1$

Here *a* and *b* are features and it is assumed that some condition
guarantees that each $S\langle b\rangle$ has a Conj node as immediate constituent. The interpretation of schemata like (7) is that the

variable n ranges over positive integers greater than 1, so that (7) is a simple proof-theoretic system that constructs a countably infinite set of phrase structure *rules*.

Of course, under the standard interpretation of such schemata, they are completely incapable of characterizing any coordinate compounds of transfinite length, including all those with degrees of branching of transfinite cardinality. Suppose one tried to remedy this via the following interpretation, which we call *pseudo-constructive*. Let the variable n in schemata like (7) range not only over positive integers, but also over transfinite cardinal numbers. Under this interpretation, such schemata characterize not countably infinite sets of finite rules, but megacollections of rules, transfinitely many of which are of infinite size. It is a megacollection of rules which form the grammar which would actually specify the collection which is the NL to be described.

Since the rules of the grammar form a megacollection, no finite specification of an NL has been achieved. At best then, another grammar, a metagrammar (hypergrammar) is required. That is, the schema (7) only gives the illusion of being a well-defined finite specification of the grammatical rules necessary for constructing the megacollection of coordination constructions. But to interpret (7) precisely, the schematic variable n, which ranges over all cardinal numbers, finite and transfinite, must be eliminated. As Langendoen (1976: 15) puts it:

> Obviously, to determine the weak generative capacity of classes of infinite grammars, one must take into consideration more than just the types of rules contained in those grammars. One must also consider the types of devices that are used to construct the rules of those grammars, which the schemata indirectly represent. To determine what those devices are, one cannot simply consider rule schemata as abbreviatory conventions, analogous to the finite abbreviatory conventions represented by the use of curly braces and parentheses. Rather they must be thought of as standing for rules of another grammar, which enumerate all but finitely many of the rules of the infinite grammars that they are part of.

How are the rules of the metagrammar relevant to (7) to be specified? There are two choices. Either they are specified non-constructively or pseudoconstructively. If specified pseudoconstructively, then the rules of the metagrammar also form a megacollection. Thus, another grammar, a meta-metagrammar is required to specify them. Again, the rules of a meta-metagrammar may be specified either pseudoconstructively or non-constructively, and, if the former, they too form a mega-collection.

Let use define informally the notion *Indirect NL Specification System*, as a finite, non-null sequence of grammars $\langle G_1, ..., G_n \rangle$ such that (i) G_1 specifies an NL and (ii) each $G_j (j > 1)$ specifies the rules of G_{j-1} and (iii) G_n is finite. The discussion of the previous paragraph then shows that G_n must be non-constructive and cannot be pseudoconstructive. But, obviously, unless there is some substantive reason, one should provide an Indirect NL Specification System for an NL of the maximally simple sort: with $G_n = G_1$. No substantive reason for avoiding the simplest system is known. Consequently, Occam's razor rejects Indirect NL Specification Systems with pseudoconstructive grammars and metagrammars as an alternative to the directly non-constructive specification of NLs themselves.

5.3 Effability

Katz (1972, 1978, 1981) has argued that NLs manifest a property he refers to as *effability*, stated in Katz (1981: 226) as:

(E) Each proposition (thought) is expressible by some sentence in every natural language.

Katz (1981: 239) goes on to elucidate the principle (E) as follows:

... (E) makes a further claim about the completeness of the logical and expressive sides of natural languages, namely that the semantic structure of natural languages is complete with respect to the full range of objects to which laws of logic apply and that the expressive structure is complete with respect to the stock of senses semantic structure supplies.

Katz uses the term 'proposition' broadly to cover not only the meanings of declaratives, but also those of imperatives, interrogatives, etc. For convenience, we restrict attention to the subcase where 'proposition' designates senses to which truth values can sensibly be directly associated.

Katz assumed that the collection of propositions forms a recursively enumerable set, properly observing (1978: 224–5) that this meant that many facts could not have a description in any proposition:

> One consequence of effability is that the class of propositions has the cardinality of the natural numbers. The set of sentences of a natural language has the cardinality of the natural numbers, and since propositions are senses of sentences and the number of senses of a sentence is finite, the propositions must be of the same cardinality as the sentences ... Accordingly, one might claim that a deep ineffability still remains. The cardinality of the realm of facts would seem to be higher than that of the propositions, since presumably for each real number it is a *fact* that that real number is a number (less than some other number). There thus seems to remain an 'ineffability' in the relation of facts to propositions, namely, not every such fact is described in some proposition which states just that fact; some elude conceptual representation.

Thus for Katz, there are three realms, only the first two of which turn out to be equinumerous: sentence senses (propositions), sentence forms, and facts. The former two have the cardinality $\aleph_0$, while the realm of facts is a megacollection.

A different view had already in effect been argued by Russell (1903: 367):

> Or again, take the class of propositions. Every object can occur in some proposition, and it seems indubitable that there are at least as many propositions as there are objects. For, if u be a fixed class, 'x is a u' will be a different proposition for every different value of x ... But classes of propositions are only some among objects, yet Cantor's argument shows that there are more of them than there are propositions.

For Russell, 'object' was a term with maximally wide reference. Any entity, concrete or abstract, could be referred to by an instantiation of the variable 'x' in his remarks, including arbitrary *sets*.

But Cantor's argument, to which Russell referred, had already shown that the realm of sets was a megacollection, and hence not only that the collection covered by 'x' in Russell's remarks was bigger than a recursively enumerable set, but bigger than any set whatever. Hence implicit in Russell's remarks is the view that there is a megacollection of propositions. There is then no reason to assume that any fact lacks an associated proposition (in fact, many) to characterize it. The only way to avoid this conclusion would be to adopt a syntactic view of proposition and to claim that such syntactic objects are subject to a first-order transfinite size law, that is, an analogue of (2) of chapter 3. But the objections to this arbitrary decision are the same as those directed earlier toward analogous size laws in the realm of NL sentences and NL coordinate compounds.

Looked at in this way, Katz's account can be reinterpreted as a novel argument that NLs are megacollections of sentences:

(8) a. There is, as Russell indicated, a megacollection of propositions, at least one for each fact.
     b. Each proposition is, according to Katz's effability principle, a sense of some sentence of each NL.
     c. The collection of senses associated with each NL sentence is a set.[9]

---

[9] (8c) is a weakening of Katz's claim that no sentence has more than a finite number of senses. The need for a weakening is shown by sentences with infinitely many ambiguous conjuncts. If only at most finitely many of these ambiguities cancel out, the resulting compound sentences are infinitely ambiguous. If the claim were weakened to the point that a single sentence could be associated with a megacollection of senses, the argument in (8) simply would not go through. However, there is no reason to weaken the claim to that extent, a weakening which would make it impossible to take sentences to be sets and hence impossible to take NLs to be collections of sentences. Moreover, the hypothetical 'language' once suggested by B. Partee, consisting of a single sentence which expresses every proposition, seems a dubious candidate for NL-hood.

Restriction (8c) is simply a special case of the following replacement for the standard view that each sentence is a finite object:

(i) Each NL sentence is a set of linguistic entities (relations, etc.).

This claims that while NLs as wholes are megacollections, each individual sentence has a fixed cardinality along every dimension. A weaker claim than (i) would make it impossible to speak of an individual sentence as an element of a collection.

    d.   Hence the collection of propositions and the collection of sentences of any NL are equinumerous.

    e.   Consequently, each NL contains a megacollection of sentences.

The claim that the collection of propositions is a megacollection can be approached slightly differently, via the argument for the NL Vastness Theorem in (15). There we saw that the collection of sentences in an NL with coordinate compounding of sentences is a megacollection. Each element of the megacollection of declarative sentences of an NL expresses a proposition, just as the basic (non-compound) declarative sentences do. Since a coordinate compound declarative sentence expresses a proposition distinct from any of the propositions expressed by its component subconjuncts (see Frege (1977)), the megacollection of declarative sentences of an NL must express a megacollection of distinct propositions.

Consequently, Katz's effability principle (E) would necessarily be false if NLs were restricted to sets of sentences of any fixed cardinality (finite or transfinite). But the effability thesis remains viable if maximal collections of Nl sentences, like the collection of propositions itself, are megacollections. Thus one positive consequence of the NL Vastness Theorem is that it keeps the effability principle consistent with the magnitude of the collection of propositions. There is then no known basis for believing that there is any limitation whatever on the expressive power of NLs, nothing whatever which can be said about any of the megacollection of facts which the *structure of NLs* prevents from being expressed. Thus, the NL Vastness Theorem shows that NLs have a grandeur which even Katz's insightful discussions of effability had partially denied them.

Our remarks here amount to a denial that the following claim by Putnam (1975a: 327) holds for NLs: 'But it is a theorem of set theory that *no* language L *can* contain names for *all* the collections of things that could be formed, at least not if the number of things is infinite.'

Presumably, the theorem referred to is just that the power set of an infinite set S has a greater cardinality than S. To apply Putnam's conclusion to NLs then would require the assumption that the collection of NL expressions is a set, say a countably infinite set. But this assumption is refuted by the NL Vastness Theorem. Putnam (1975a) gave no argument for the view that NLs are (countably infinite) sets, simply stating the standard unargued assumption that they are (1975a: 14):

> Since 'sets' are identified with predicates taken in extension in the system of *Principia*, there are then non-denumerably many pair-wise noncoextensive predicates of integers. However, there are only denumerably many well formed formulas in *Principia*. Hence, *the huge majority of all predicates of integers must be indefinable* (in the system of *Principia*, and indeed in any human language or constructed system).

With respect to NLs, Putnam's conclusion is nothing more than the unsupported and false view that each NL sentence is finite. With respect to the formulas in *Principia*, the assumption holds by definition of the system. Putnam failed to distinguish here a conclusion about the formulas of the system in *Principia*, which holds by virtue of the *stipulations* of its constructors (B. Russell and A. Whitehead) and a conclusion about NLs, which can only be justified by an *argument*.

The observation of Frege's cited above that a declarative coordinate compound expresses a proposition distinct from those expressed by its components is related to a matter touched on in section 3.3: the claim that transfinite sentences share the defining structural features of finite sentences. These structural features include logico-semantic properties. In particular, the truth value of a *finite* compound of declaratives is a function of the truth value of the component subconjuncts. For the case where the member of Conj is a particle equivalent to logical 'and', the whole compound is true if and only if each of the component subconjuncts is. This principle is a truth of any valid formulation of propositional logic. But exactly this principle generalizes to *transfinite* coordinate compounds. Clearly, a coordinate compound with e.g. $\aleph_0$ conjuncts is true if and only if each of the infinitely many component subconjuncts is true. The principles relevant for disjunctive compounding also evidently generalize to transfinite coordinate compounds. It would be entirely arbitrary and generalization-missing to limit formulation of the relevant principles of propositional logic to any subcase determined by an arbitrary size bound on the number of conjuncts. But since the logic which applies to finite compounds applies to transfinite compounds, it would, from this distinct point of view, be entirely unjustified to deny the latter sentencehood merely because of their size. Hence the logical properties of transfinite coordinate compounds support the view that they are NL sentences, since they obey the logical laws of finite NL sentences.

5.4   Language learning

NLs are presumably called 'natural' because human beings appear to be able to learn the ones they are exposed to as children naturally – that is, spontaneously and without special instruction – unlike certain artificial languages, which children cannot learn without special instruction. The past twenty years or so have seen the development of theories of NL learning designed to explain the specific ability of human beings to learn NLs. These theories take as their starting point the observation that when children are presented with small samples of NL input, they develop the ability to form judgements about the grammatical status and properties of much larger collections of sentences of those NLs. Limitations of time, computing space and storage space aside, it is assumed that people are able to judge the grammatical status and properties of any sentence whatever of the NLs they have learned. It is further assumed that the ability to judge the grammatical status and properties of the sentences of NLs based on acquiring finite characterizations of those NLs. Given that NLs are not finite, the same reasoning that led to the claim that theories of NLs must be generative grammars (see chapter 2) led to the claim that the characterization of NLs that people acquire must also be generative grammars (Miller and Chomsky (1963: 466–7); Chomsky (1965: 4); Wexler and Culicover (1980: 33)).

A grammar of an NL J is simply a set of necessary and sufficient conditions for sentencehood in J. A generative grammar is, moreover, one which not only provides such conditions but also provides a procedure for generating (constructing) each sentence. Following Bever (1982: 440), let us designate as a *psychogrammar* a grammar which is mentally represented in some (human) being. We say that P *is a psychogrammar of J* if and only if the range of P includes all the sentences of J known by a speaker of J.

Questions about language learning are questions about psychogrammars and hence, in our terms, are part of psychology and not linguistics. Nonetheless, linguistic conclusions can and do bear on such questions. In particular, the NL Vastness Theorem entails that NLs cannot be generated, a conclusion which determines the NL Non-constructivity Theorem, which specifies that no NL has any generative grammar. Consider then the assumption that underlies almost all current work in the study of human NL acquisition:

(9)   To learn a particular NL is to learn a grammar that generates it.

(9) is equivalent to:

(10)   Let L be an NL. Then, if P is a psychogrammar of L, P is generative.

But the NL Non-constructivity Theorem determines that (10) is false.

(11)   *The Psychogrammar Theorem*
       THEOREM: Let P be a generative psychogrammar of L and let J be an NL. Then: $J \neq L$.
       Proof: Immediate from the NL Non-constructivity Theorem.

This theorem leaves only the following possibilities with respect to human knowledge of K, where K is (i) an NL and (ii) such that there are attested sentences of K (that is, as one says, K 'has speakers'). Either the speakers of K have learned K in its entirety or they have not, that is, speakers of K have learned a psychogrammar P of K or they have not. If the former, P is a finite non-constructive grammar, which gives the conditions for sentencehood in K but which does not provide a procedure for generating all the sentences of K. If the latter, then P is a non-constructive grammar with a size law that limits the characterized sentences to some subset of elements all smaller than the size limit or a constructive grammar with or without a (finite) size law. In the former case, the subset of characterized sentences is a set whose cardinality remains undetermined so far. In the latter case, the subset of characterized sentences is either a countably infinite or finite set.

These are merely the logical possibilities allowed by the Psychogrammar Theorem. If examined from the point of factual plausibility however, only two really survive. There is no more reason to believe that psychogrammars include finite size laws than linguistic grammars per se. Consequently, the surviving positions are (i) P is a generative grammar with no finite size law, hence one specifying a recursively enumerable set of cardinality $\aleph_0$; or (ii) P is a non-constructive grammar with no size law specifying a megacollection. In the former case, P is not a grammar of an NL and speakers of K cannot be said to know K but only part of K. In the latter case, P is an NL grammar and speakers of K in principle know K in its entirety.

The psycholinguistic question of whether P is a generative grammar or a non-constructive grammar cannot be decided on any known basis so far. However, no known considerations, either linguistic or psychological, indicate that P need be generative, as so far assumed in work on such matters. That is, it is entirely *possible* that human beings internally represent (non-constructive) systems which *fully* characterize the megacollections which are NLs. This would mean that it makes as much sense to say that human beings know all members of such a megacollection as it does to say they know each of the members of some presumed infinite recursively enumerable set.[10]

The claim that the megacollection property of NLs is perfectly compatible with human knowledge of NLs follows from nothing more than the feasability of *finite* non-constructive characterizations of megacollections, one approach to which was outlined in section 2. However, this result does clash with what has been a

---

[10] But we agree with Katz (1981) that it makes little sense to speak this way. More generally, a relation 'knowing a grammar' must be entirely different from a relation 'knowing a sentence', despite Chomsky's (1980a: 69–70) conflation of them. To know a particular sentence involves forming actual intuitions about it, e.g. that it is ambiguous, end rhymes with some other, etc. In this sense, no speaker can know more than a relatively small finite set of sentences, even if (s)he has internally represented a grammar which characterizes a megacollection. Talk about 'knowing' a grammar can only be confusing, because no one claims to have actual intuitions about grammars. If humans had such, grammatical study would be a quite different, and probably much easier field of investigation. The absence of such intuitions is a fact about people, not about grammars or NLs.

pervasive *myth* about linguistic knowledge throughout the development of generative grammar, one which has defined the conceptual foundations of much of the work in this area. This myth is already represented by the quote in section 2.1 from Chomsky (1959), analyzed in our (1) of that section. The basic idea is that a finite representation of an infinite collection must be a constructive, proof-theoretic device. Formulated specifically with reference to linguistic knowledge, the myth runs something like this:

(12)   a.   NLs are infinite sets.
       b.   Human beings know (learn) these infinite sets.
       c.   Human minds/brains are finite.
       d.   Therefore, there must exist generative grammars, finite
            constructive devices, represented in human minds
            which account for this knowledge.

This doctrine, some version of which is ubiquitous in discussions of the underlying assumptions of generative grammar, is seen in such passages as the following from Lees (1965: 42–3):

> ... and since ... each brain contains only a finite amount of 'storage space' available for any sentences which might have been heard and memorized, it seems quite reasonable to suppose that a speaker makes up new sentences according to some fixed finite set of rules ... These rules would serve, presumably, to enumerate the sentences. Thus, if we are ever to formulate some reasonable theory of language which accounts for these facts, we must believe that the set of sentences is at least recursively enumerable, even if it turns out not to be recursive.

The fallacious assumption here is, of course, the view that any fixed, finite well-defined principles characterizing an infinite collection must be *constructive* and hence must characterize a recursively enumerable set. The remarks simply ignore the possibility of non-constructive characterizations of collections.

The assumptions underlying Lees' remarks are similar to those found in the claim by Langendoen (1964: 14):

> This position has recently been put forward by Chomsky as capturing the essence of sentence formation in any language:

there is no numerical bound on the number of sentences of a
language, whereas the number of rules of grammar is necessarily finite. Therefore, certain of these rules must, in the
derivation of particular sentences, apply arbitrarily many
times, ...

The conclusion beginning with 'Therefore' here is a non-sequitur,
since there is no necessity for a (non-constructive) grammar to
involve any notion of rules as operations, as 'applying', etc. A
non-psychological statement of the fallacy under discussion is provided by Hockett (1966: 187):

More specifically, however, we require that a harp [set of
strings], if it is infinite, be at least *recursively enumerable*.
This is really equivalent to saying that we do not recognize a
set as a harp unless it can be characterized by a finite
grammar.

The assumption underlying the remarks by Chomsky, Lees,
Langendoen and Hockett, and which was unquestioned in the
generative framework, is the unargued doctrine that a finite characterization of an infinite collection must *logically* be a set of
operations, that is, a Turing-machine equivalent. Since this is just
not the case, as the classical appeal to non-constructive characterizations of collections in set theory and mathematics should have
made clear, the argument in (12) from the acceptable assumptions
(12a, b, c) to (12d) is in significant part a non-sequitur.
  Given the NL Vastness Theorem, the validity of the entailment
from (12a, b, c) to (12d) would have revealed that in principle
human beings cannot learn NLs in their entirety. Since no such
entailment holds, however, even the severe basic limitations on
human linguistic knowledge are not at all known to be incompatible with the learning of a system which would provide knowledge
of a megacollection, to the extent that it makes sense to speak of
knowledge of infinite systems. Humans could simply learn a non-
constructive psychogrammar characterizing a megacollection. Of
course, it is logically possible that some argument distinct from
(12) could show that the megacollections of NLs are not fully
finitely representable, even non-constructively. This would indicate that *full* knowledge of NLs by humans or any finite automaton is impossible. Although we see no reason to expect that this

will ever be shown, it does highlight the point that once one makes the necessary distinction between NLs and knowledge of NLs (see chapter 6), the possibility arises that humans might not have full knowledge of the former.

Suppose for purposes of discussion that psychogrammars are non-constructive NL grammars; that is, that people learn the NLs to which they are exposed as children, not merely parts of those NLs. From this, it does not follow, as is commonly assumed, that every NL can be learned (see Wexler and Culicover (1980: 1)). Because of limitations on time, computing space and storage space, not every NL is learnable; see section 6.4. Nor, for reasons touched on in section 7.5, is every NL identifiable in the limit in the sense of Gold (1967).[11] However, the barriers to human learning of an NL have to do not with the size of that NL itself but with the size of the smallest adequate inductive basis of that NL (see section 3.3). NLs do not have to be finite, finite-state, context-free, context-sensitive, recursive or recursively enumerable sets to be learnable. Hence the NL Vastness Theorem does not create any crisis in the domain of NL learnability.

Continuing to suppose that psychogrammars are non-constructive, we may nonetheless assume that human beings possess certain constructive devices relevant to speaking and understanding. For, as has been rightly stressed throughout the history of generative grammar, even what we are calling psychogrammars are *not* models for either speaker or hearer. That is, psychogrammars are neither devices for finding well-formed expressions for semantic objects nor parsers which, inter alia, find the semantic objects associated with a given expression; see Chomsky (1965: 9ff). Nonetheless, it is reasonably assumed that human beings are equipped with both types of mechanism, and such devices are not even well-defined without access to a psychogrammar. However, these devices are reasonably thought of as computational or algorithmic. It is plausible, therefore, that even though NLs are megacollections and their grammars thus necessarily non-constructive, certain purely constructive principles are built into the structured systems of human linguistic performance.

---

[11] A language is identifiable in the limit if it is learned upon exposure to a finite number of sentences presented serially. Thus this concept in effect generalizes learnability by eliminating normal time constraints.

These would then only be able to deal in principle with a sub-collection of all NL sentences, conceivably finite, but perhaps an infinite recursively enumerable set. Such speculations are entirely consistent with both the NL Vastness Theorem and the Psycho-grammar Theorem.

The remarks just made about sentences capable of actual use lead to the following observations connecting the NL Vastness Theorem with past linguistic work. While NLs are mega-collections, there is a subcollection made up of all and only the finite sentences in each NL. Such subcollections are, moreover, sets. Clearly, nothing precludes inquiry into the properties of these sets. For instance, Pullum's and Gazdar's (1982) study of the context-free character of NL string-sets shows that the existing arguments for their non-context-free character are all flawed. While not concluding that NLs involve context-free string-sets, they do ask why it is, at the least, so hard to demonstrate their non-context-free character if it does hold. The NL Vastness Theorem has, of course, shown that NLs as such are not coexten-sive with context-free string-sets, since they are not coextensive with any sets at all. But this leaves entirely open whether the string-set associated with the subcollection of all and only the *finite* sentences in some NL is context-free. All other possible mathematical, linguistic and psychological questions about such subcollections also survive. It must only be understood that their answers concern only *parts* of NLs, albeit important parts, and not NLs themselves. An analogy with Cantor's results should be obvious. The fact that Cantor's work led to a hierarchy of sets of infinite size and to the recognition of megacollections in no way impeded study of countably infinite or recursively enumerable sets. The NL Vastness Theorem does not require valid results about the collection of finite sentences to be discarded. It only limits the way they can be interpreted. Inquiry into the properties of the computable subset of an NL is surely of psychological relevance. It just should not be confused with grammatical study proper, any more than size-bounded computer arithmetic should be confused with the principles of number theory.

6

Ontological Escape Hatches

6.0 Remarks

As noted at the outset, this study derives in part from Katz's critique of the now standard ontological position in linguistics that grammars and grammatical theory characterize a psychological domain, and his extensive argument (Katz (1981, 1983)) for the view that NLs are abstract (platonic) objects, not psychological ones. Despite this, we presented the argument for the mega-collection character of NLs in something of an ontological vacuum. In particular, we have not considered whether ontological commitments themselves could provide some justified basis for rejecting the applicability of the NL Vastness Theorem to NLs, even while granting its validity. That is, we have not asked whether ontological commitments could offer grounds for rejecting the truth of key principles of the argument, specifically the pivotal claims that NLs involve sentences of infinite size and that NLs are closed under coordinate compounding. We now turn to this issue directly, with the aim of showing that there is no justifiable escape from the NL Vastness Theorem via appeal to the ontological underpinnings of linguistic research.

6.1 Ontological positions about universals

The conclusions that the collections of sentences forming NLs are megacollections holds only if there are sentences of infinite size (in fact, of all transfinite sizes). Do underlying ontological assumptions offer any way of rejecting this view, thus rendering the formally valid proof of the NL Vastness Theorem inapplicable to NLs? To aid consideration of this issue, it will be helpful to consider four distinct 'putative objects', where by 'putative object' we mean something which might a priori be part of some aspect of reality:

(1) a. the set of all sets
    b. (i) Babar is happy and I know that Babar is happy.
      (ii) Babar is $happy_1$ and I know that Babar is $happy_2$ and I know that I know that Babar is $happy_3$ ... and ... $happy_k$.
      (iii) Babar is $happy_1$ and I know that Babar is $happy_2$ and I know that I know that Babar is $happy_3$ ... and ... $happy_{\aleph_0}$.

There are three distinguishable ontological views with respect to the existence of objects that are of relevance here. These views are characterized as follows by Fraenkel, Bar-Hillel and Levy (1973: 331–2):

> Our first problem regards the ontological status of sets – not of this or the other set, but of sets in general. Since sets, as ordinarily understood, are what philosophers call *universals*, our present problem is part of the well-known and amply discussed classical problem of the *ontological status of the universals*. The three main traditional answers to the general problem of universals ... are known as *realism, nominalism,* and *conceptualism*.

See also Quine (1953: 14). Katz (1981: 22) relates these traditional views to linguistics as follows:

> We can reasonably expect that the range of possible answers to these questions about the foundations of linguistics will be the same as the range for parallel questions about the foundations of other sciences. Looking at the possible answers to the parallel questions in the foundations of mathematics, logic, physics, psychology and the other special sciences, we find that the range of answers that have been given derives from, and is limited by, the range of positions on the nature

of universals in traditional metaphysics. Thus, we find Platonic realism, conceptualism, and nominalism, together with their various particular forms. Platonic realism holds that universals are real but distinct from physical or mental objects (i.e., non-spatial, non-temporal, and independent of minds). Conceptualism holds that universals are mental, with its particular forms arising from different specifications of the sense of 'mental'. Nominalism holds that only the sensible signs of language are real; the alleged use of them to name universals is nothing more than reference to space-time particulars with signs that apply generally on the basis of resemblance.

If one considers what these positions say about the putative entities in (1), one can initially be sure that, today, no ontological position can countenance the reality of the putative object characterized in (1a) since, as the set-theoretical paradoxes show, the notion is not consistent. Hence all positions will agree that simply is no set of all sets.

Turn then to objects of greater linguistic relevance. (1bi) is a finite coordinate sentence and, moreover, one small in size. It is short enough to actually be used (produced, understood) by actual human beings. All three ontological positions can accept such a putative object as a real linguistic object. Nominalists can take (1bi) as real because they can try to view it as a physical object, identifying it with, say, the noise produced when it is articulated, or perhaps the articulatory gestures which produce the noise, or perhaps some physical goings on in the brain which are related to these gestures. Crucial for the nominalist is that any putative universal be reducible to individuals and hence, in the case of NLs, presumably to physical particulars; and this is at least conceivable for cases like (1bi).

The conceptualist and platonist also have no problems in accepting (1bi) as a real linguistic object, although obviously their interpretations of the nature of this reality differ and both differ from the nominalist interpretation. For the conceptualist, (1bi) is linguistically real because it is an aspect of the linguistic part of the psychological structure of real human beings, for instance, something truly characterized by a psychologically real grammar. Its reality can be construed as being in the range of the output of a psychologically real Turing machine (generative psycho-grammar). For the platonist, (1bi) is also real, but it has the reality of any other abstract object. The presence or absence of any psychologically real grammar is irrelevant to the platonist exis-tence of (1bi) just as the existence or not of any psychologically real principles of arithmetic is irrelevant to the platonist existence of integers.

While it is possible to raise and settle ontological issues relevant to linguistics on the basis of examples like (1bi) (see Katz (1981, 1983)), this may involve relatively extensive and complicated argu-ments, since none of the three positions is *immediately* embar-rassed by such cases. The issues become sharper, though, in the case of putative objects like (1bii). This is intended to represent a sentence which involves k conjuncts, each consisting of an initial sequence of *I know that* ... arranged in increasing length. The number k, which gives the cardinality of the conjuncts, is, however, enormous. For concreteness, think of it as ten to the millionth power. Thus, while (1bii) is a finite putative object, it is so large that there is no possibility of it being produced/understood etc. by any human being, or indeed any plausible creature whatever.

Immediately then, it is difficult to see how to interpret (1bii) as a real linguistic object in a frankly nominalistic ontology. There simply is no real noise, sequence of articulatory gestures, or collec-tion of brain activities which can be associated with such a huge construct; moreover, there is not even any potential utterance or articulation to fill this role, if by 'potential' one means really pro-ducible by a human being. Hence a consistent nominalism should reject the existence of examples like (1bii) and, more generally, should claim that NLs are finite collections of (relatively short) sentences. For the nominalist, the notion of unperformable sen-tences does not make any sense. Put differently, in nominalist terms, distinct sentence tokens can be taken to represent the same sentence type only by meeting *physical criteria of similarity*. Sen-tence types cannot exist without corresponding sets of tokens.

Since the imposition of a nominalist ontology on linguistics is incompatible even with the existence of huge finite sentences, it is of course also incompatible with the existence of transfinite sen-tences. The mere ontological equation of sentence with something physical suffices to provide a principled basis for rejecting the existence of transfinite sentences. Hence, *if* a nominalist approach to linguistics were viable in general, this would offer a genuine ontological basis for rejecting the assumptions necessary to render the NL Vastness Theorem relevant to NLs.

However, maintenance of a nominalist interpretation of linguistic reality is out of the question. The most obvious and basic feature of sentences and NLs cannot even be discussed, still less explained, in such terms. If the position is taken literally, it makes no sense to talk about sentential properties like syntactic well-formedness, synonymy, phonotactic well-formedness, ambiguity, etc. For none of these is definable in terms of physical structures. Under a nominalist view, linguistics must reduce to the physics of human utterances, to the neurophysiology of the human vocal apparatus, or to some sort of neurophysics of brains. Since such conclusions amount to a reductio of the position, no viable attack on the NL Vastness Theorem can be formulated on such a basis. As Katz (1981) considers in some detail, it seems correct to conclude that the early generative grammar (conceptualist) critique of the essentially nominalist foundations of pre-1957 American structural linguistics provides more than sufficient grounds for rejecting any nominalist position in linguistics, a position which, moreover, is not clearly maintained currently by anyone. See Postal (1966) for a critique of one attempted nominalist interpretation of linguistics.

Unlike the nominalist view, the conceptualist position encounters no particular problems with large finite sentences such as (1bii).[1] They can be said to have the same reality as short sentences such as (1bi): they fall within the (infinite) range of a finite psychogrammar. Hence a conceptualist interpretation of linguistic reality, unlike a nominalistic approach, is not limited to taking NLs to be finite collections and is not committed to the view that every NL sentence is performable. The conceptualist can assume that just as most arithmetical computations are too large to be actually carried out by any fixed automaton, human or not, so most NL sentences are too large to be actually performed. But, since conceptualism need not require that real objects be physical

---

[1] Although the conceptualist position in general encounters no such difficulties, particular formulations of it may and do; see section 3.

objects,[2] the unperformability of most NL sentences has no consequences for their reality.

Similarly, in platonist terms, the size of infinite sentences is clearly irrelevant to their existence. Moreover, not only does the platonist view not require any physical characterization of real sentences, it also does not require that they be within the range of any *psychologically* real grammar (psychogrammar).[3] So huge sentences like (1bii) raise no issues for the platonist interpretation of linguistic reality.

We turn then to structures like (1biii), intended to represent a sentence of a huge number of clauses, formed exactly like (1bii), *except* that the number of conjuncts is the infinite cardinal $\aleph_0$. As already indicated, a nominalist ontology obviously rejects (1biii), which has no possible physical interpretation. But, given the untenability of a nominalist ontology in linguistics, this has no relevance to present concerns. Even in platonist terms, a putative object can fail to be a real object. This happens when the characterization of the putative object is not well-defined or, as for (1a), when the characterization is not consistent. But the platonist position is receptive to the existence of any universals whose characterizations lack these defects. Since denumerably infinite sized sentences such as (1biii) are perfectly well-defined and subject to no known contradiction, the platonist ontological position takes them as real. Moreover, they are taken as real *linguistic* objects since they share the (non-size) properties of unquestioned linguistic objects of finite size. It follows that transfinite sentences are perfectly possible under a platonist conception, which does not linguistically differentiate such sentences from huge finite ones, or, for that matter, from finite ones small enough to be attested (known, performed, understood). The interesting questions relating transfinite sentences to ontological issues thus concern their connection with the conceptualist position.

One point of importance is the question of justification of any

[2] We take conceptualism to have distinct variants, some of which claim psychological reality can be reduced to physical reality, others of which do not. This bifurcation is not relevant to our concerns.

[3] Of course, the platonist view of NLs and NL grammars is not incompatible with the existence of psychologically real grammars, any more than the platonist view of number theory is incompatible with computers.

conceptualist position in linguistics as against a platonist position. Even if it could be shown that one or another conceptualist interpretation of linguistic reality could justifiably exclude transfinite sentences, which we deny, this would only be a truly significant result if, in addition, there were serious grounds for choosing a conceptualist ontology for linguistics rather than, in particular, a platonist one. In fact, the question does not seem to have ever been seriously addressed. Chomsky (1980a: 28–30) considers platonist linguistics to be the study of 'languages as such' and not the study of 'human language', and for that reason dismisses it. But there is no basis for his position, since the notion 'human language', which is equivalent to our notion NL, can certainly be studied within platonist linguistics. See also Katz (1981: 46) for further criticism of this passage of Chomsky's.

In so far as conceptualists have attempted to justify their view of linguistic reality, they have essentially limited themselves to arguing its superiority to one or another nominalistic approach. As Katz (1981: 84) remarks:

> Chomsky's argument for conceptualism, ..., contains no reasons to show that psychological constraints are adequate but only reasons to show that they are more adequate than nominalist ones. Hence, the emergence of Platonism – which places neither physicalist nor psychological constraints on theories in linguistics – makes it necessary for the justification of conceptualism to go beyond Chomsky's argument. The onus of proof is on the conceptualist to demonstrate why psychological constraints ought not to be considered an ad hoc and unnecessary imposition.

Chomsky (1980b: 43) had a clear opportunity to justify his conceptualism as against a platonist view sketched with some clarity by critics of the fragments of his *Rules and Representations* published in *The Behavior and Brain Sciences*. In their comments on these fragments, Cummins and Harnish (1980: 18) stated:

> We are puzzled as to why Chomsky is puzzled when he writes: 'What is "psychological reality" as distinct from "truth in a certain domain"?' and 'Why didn't [Sapir's] "linguistic evidence" suffice to establish "psychological reality"?' If linguistics is about the mind, or one of its faculties – if it is

about psychological states – then, of course, evidence for the truth of the theory is evidence of psychological reality. But linguistic evidence itself can't tell us whether linguistics is about the mind, and that's the issue – subject matter – that linguistics is *about*. The 'psychological reality' dispute boils down to this: should the theoretical terms playing an essential role in the results of linguistic analysis and description be interpreted as about mental states or not? After all, most practicing linguists were brought up on the following words:

> From now on I will consider a language to be a set (finite or infinite) of sentences, each finite in length and constructed out of a finite set of elements ... The grammar of L will thus be a device that generates all of the grammatical sequences of L and none of the ungrammatical ones (Chomsky (1957, p. 13)).

Theories of language constructed to the letter (and in the spirit) of such remarks need no more be about the mind than a piece of set theory is ... Chomsky's puzzlement about the 'psychological reality' issue strongly suggests that he thinks there is no alternative to supposing that linguistics is psychology. And it seems clear that he thinks this because he is a 'conceptualist' about language – i.e. because he thinks there is no such thing as a natural language independent of speakers' psychological states, hence nothing for a non-psychologized linguistics to be about.'

Instead of offering some justification for his conceptualism, which Cummins and Harnish were properly requesting and which Katz had noted to be previously non-existent, Chomsky (1980b: 43) would say nothing more than:

> Perhaps C&H are taking the position that such facts as the 'sample facts' could be facts about 'English' (an infinite system) even if there were no representation of knowledge of English in the minds of speaker-hearers (or anywhere). They do not try to develop this possibility, so I will not pursue it.

Because Katz (1981, 1983) has now presented just such a development in great detail, even if it had been justified for Chomsky to avoid supporting his conceptualism against platonism before, that possibility has now certainly vanished. Since Katz (1981, 1983) presents an extensive justification of the platonist interpretation as against any conceptual interpretation, continued failure to refute Katz's position and failure to support the conceptualist position can only leave the latter as merely an extensively socially institutionalized, but intellectually unjustified approach to linguistics.

These remarks about the relative justification of conceptualism and platonism indicate that in what follows we are undertaking a task which is, strictly speaking, not currently necessary. We show that even if one adopts a conceptualist position, there is no justifiable way to exclude transfinite sentences from NLs. But there is no known grounded basis for accepting any conceptualist framework since (i) no such framework has ever been seriously defended against the platonist position as a basis for linguistics and (ii) Katz (1981, 1983) presents a well-developed body of arguments for the superiority of a platonist viewpoint over any possible conceptualism.

Ignoring now the question of justification for a conceptualist ontology, we ask whether anything internal to this framework justifiably excludes transfinite sentences from the linguistic realm. It is uncertain whether principles *inherent* to a conceptualist interpretation of linguistics *in general* are compatible with the view that (1biii), for example, is an element of an NL. There is no initial reason why this sentence cannot be accorded the same sort of reality as (1bi) or (1bii). That is, it could be in the range of objects characterized by a psychologically real grammar. The only necessity is that this psychogrammar be non-constructive. The psychological interpretation of grammars *in itself* does not require that mentally represented grammars be constructive. To the almost total extent that this has so far been assumed in the literature (see, for example, the quotes from Lees in chapter 2 and from Langendoen and Lees in section 5.4), the view has been unjustified, in particular, unjustified by the mere commitment to a conceptualist ontology.

6.2   Standard conceptualism

There are particular versions, formulations or interpretations of the conceptualist position which, however, might seem to determine a rejection of the existence of (1biii). For instance, suppose, following Chomsky's well-known view, the claim that human beings develop psychologically real internalized grammars is interpreted such that these psychogrammars characterize *knowledge of NLs*. As Chomsky (1977b: 81) puts it:

> For our purposes we can think of a language as a set of structural descriptions of sentences, where a full structural description determines (in particular) the sound and meaning of a linguistic expression. Knowledge of a language can be expressed in the form of a system of rules (a grammar) that generates the language.

Such a view means that a person possessing an internally represented grammar has, *in principle*, knowledge of each sentence of the NL characterized by that grammar. Since the views Chomsky expresses in this passage have become very dominant in contemporary linguistics, we will refer to this version of the overall conceptualist position as *standard conceptualism*. Under this view, both NLs and their grammars are taken to be real objects, and, by internalizing $G(NL_i)$, a child gains knowledge of NL_i, that is, knowledge in principle of each sentence of NL_i. We see in section 4 that, starting about 1980, Chomsky himself has abandoned standard conceptualism for a new, though still conceptualist, position.

Suppose further that, within standard conceptualism, instantiated knowledge of a particular sentence S is provided by constructing a psychologically real internal representation of S. The difference between assuming that a psychogrammar guarantees knowledge in principle of every sentence and assuming that a speaker possessing such a grammar has instantiated knowledge of any specific sentence is crucial. It is, roughly, the difference between being able to actually mentally construct the intuition providing the knowledge about the sentence and possessing an internal system which guarantees that such an intuition could be formed *if* there were enough time, memory, computing space, etc.[4]

---

[4] Given the distinctions here, use of a single term to cover the relation between an individual and both intuitably knowable and intuitably unknowable sentences can only yield confusion. But Chomsky (1980a: 69) introduces precisely such a term: 'To avoid terminological confusion, let me introduce a technical term devised for the purpose, namely "cognize," with the following properties. The particular things we know, we also cognize. In the case of English, presented with the examples "the candidates wanted each other to win" and "the candidates

Consider (2a, b, c):

(2) a. Jack$_1$ and his father$_2$ are visiting relatives.
     b. Jack$_1$ and his father$_2$ and his father's father$_3$ are visiting relatives.
     c. Jack$_1$ and his father$_2$ and his father's father$_3$ and ... and his ... father$_k$ are visiting relatives.
     d. Jack$_1$ and his father$_2$ and his father's father$_3$ and ... and his ... father$_{\aleph_0}$ are visiting relatives.

English speakers can actually have instantiated knowledge that both (2a, b) are ambiguous. They can actually form the intuitions that these sentences specify that a certain collection of people are engaged in the activity of visiting relatives or that a certain collection of people have the property of being relatives who are visiting someone. But while a correct English grammar, interpreted in standard conceptualist terms, surely guarantees that the same properties hold for (2c), understood to have k conjuncts, with the value of k defined as for (1bii), no speaker can actually form the mental judgement about (2c) (in the way possible for (2a, b)). It seems incorrect then to claim that a speaker has direct (intuitive) instantiated knowledge of this fact about (2c). Similar remarks then hold for (2d), parallel to (2c) except in having a denumerable infinity of conjuncts.

The construction of particular intuitions could be claimed to be possible for each sentence not exceeding the computational and memory limits of the human organism because the psychogrammar is constructive, actually provides a method for forming each sentence. As Lees (1960a: 2) put it informally but graphically: 'Our attention is focussed on these rules, which provide a recipe

---

wanted me to vote for each other," we know that the former means that each wanted the other to win, and that the latter is not well-formed with the meaning that each wanted me to vote for the other. We therefore cognize these facts. Furthermore, we cognize the system of mentally represented rules from which the facts follow. That is, we cognize the grammar that constitutes the current state of our language faculty and the rules of this system as well as the principles that govern their operation. And finally we cognize the innate schematism, along with its rules, principles and conditions.' The notion *cognize* blurs a host of distinctions, failing to differentiate properties of objects about which one can directly form intuitions from those which are beyond mental operations.

for constructing English sentences.' In these terms, to know some actual particular sentence in the way one knows (2a, b) requires constructing it mentally. This is possible in principle, the standard conceptualist might claim, because the internalized grammar is exactly a recipe for such constructions. Hence, under this interpretation, it might be claimed that psychogrammars *must* be constructive to reach their basic goal, which is to characterize knowledge of sentences. Thus, while a conceptualist interpretation of linguistic reality in general might be compatible with the claim that psychogrammars are non-constructive, it might seem that the standard conceptualist view that psychogrammars must provide the basis for speakers to actually have instantiated knowledge of individual sentences requires them to be constructive.

If tenable, the above argument would offer the standard conceptualist, who adopts the Chomskyan view that grammars describe knowledge of sentences, a genuine ontological basis for rejecting the existence of infinite sentences *as elements of NLs*. The rejection would be justified precisely as follows.

(3) a. Basic Ontological Claim (common to all variants of conceptualism): grammars describe a psychological domain.

  b. Standard Conceptualist Interpretation of Ontological Claim (3a): the domain in (3a) is knowledge of (all of an infinite collection of) sentences.

  c. Instantiated knowledge of a sentence S requires the construction of a mental representation of S.

  d. To fulfil their intended function, psychogrammars must be constructive devices, to permit the construction necessitated by (3c).

  e. Thus, all NL sentences are finite.

But the argument in (3) is not tenable since, in particular, it depends on the assumption that speakers' instantiated knowledge of sentences can *only* be accounted for if speakers possess internalized *constructive* grammars. This claim has never been justified, and is, we contend, false. The inference of (3d) from (3c) does not go through because one can exhibit a method whereby (3c) could be met even though a speaker's psychogrammar is *non-*constructive.

Suppose it is granted, at least for argument, that even a non-constructive psychogrammar would by itself *fail* to provide its possessor with instantiated knowledge of the sentences the grammar characterizes. As stressed throughout the development of generative grammar, however, (see Chomsky (1965: 9)), a grammar is *not* a model of speaker or hearer. A model of a speaker is a device that, inter alia, associates with a specific meaning (semantic representation) a (set of) phonetic representation(s), while a model of a hearer is a device which, inter alia, associates with a specific phonetic representation (or, more realistically, speech signal), a specific (set of) semantic representation(s). Call the former a *producer* and the latter a *parser*. As properly stated, in e.g. Miller and Chomsky (1963: 465ff), speakers must surely be assumed to be equipped with producers and parsers. Such devices must incorporate a grammar, or else they are simply not well-defined. Miller and Chomsky (1963: 466) express this as follows:

> We are concerned with a finite device M in which are stored the rules of a generative grammar G. This device takes as its input a string x of symbols and attempts to understand it; that is to say, M tries to assign to x a certain structural description $F(x)$ – or a set $\{F_1(x), \ldots F_m(x)\}$ of syntactic descriptions in the case of a sentence x that is structurally ambiguous in *m* different ways ... We require, in particular, that M assign a structural description $F_i(x)$ to x only if the generative grammar G stored in the memory of M assigns $F_i(x)$ to x as a possible structural description.

In general, models of the speaker/hearer of an NL, L_i, must incorporate a grammar of L_i just to define the notion 'right answer' for device M with respect to L_i. But, crucially, no known considerations suggest that this function cannot be served even if the grammar incorporated in M is non-constructive. Miller and Chomsky (1963) gave no argument for their assumption that M contains in particular a *constructive* grammar.

It is surely inevitable that both producers and parsers are constructive devices, in fact, as Miller and Chomsky (1963: 466) indicate, transducers. But there is no reason why the overall device M cannot be constructive, a transducer, *even though its contained grammar is non-constructive*. There is a natural abstract account of such devices under which they are proper transducers and yet incorporate only non-constructive grammars. The idea is that the constructive features of M should be entirely separated from any particular NL grammar M might incorporate. That is, think of M particularized for a fixed NL_i as consisting of two parts, a non-constructive grammar of NL_i, $G(NL_i)$ and a Constructor. The latter is a constructive device which, given any finite NL logical structure LF, constructs all the finite NL sentences having LF as their logical structure and which, given any finite NL phonetic representation PR, constructs all the finite NL sentences having PR as their phonetic representation. In isolation then, the Constructor is, in a sense, a constructive grammar, but not of (the finite sentences of) any particular NL. Rather, it is a constructive grammar of the union of all the finite sentences of all NLs. That is, the Constructor is a constructive grammar of the maximum subset of the finite objects of the collection US of sections 3.3 and 5.2. Moreover, the constructivity of the Constructor is well-motivated, since it is intended to be part of an automaton which actually functions in real time.

This account assumes that the finite sentences of each NL form a recursively enumerable set. This factual assumption can safely be made for our argument since, if it fails, the constructivity which standard conceptualism posits must also fail; the position will then, a priori, not yield an argument for rejecting transfinite sentences. Given this, the claim that the union of all the sets of finite sentences of all NLs is recursively enumerable is warranted by the fact that recursively enumerable sets are closed under union; see the theorem in Hopcroft and Ullman (1979: 180). This theorem could fail to apply to the finite subcollections of NLs only if their finite sentences were not reducible to strings. But, given the richness of the notion of a string, this is a most implausible assumption.

Now take M in its producer function. Having incorporated a non-constructive grammar of NL_i, M functions as a Turing machine providing constructive knowledge of the sentences of NL_i as follows. Receiving some finite logical form LF as input, the Constructor M recursively enumerates, that is, actually constructs, a set of overall NL sentences. Either LF is the logical form of some finite sentence of NL_i or it is not. If it is not, the Constructor will function indefinitely without ever constructing a sentence whose logical form is LF. Assume then that M receives as inputs only meanings which are logical forms of NL_i sentences. Given Katz's effability principle from section 5.3, this is only the assumption that the inputs to M are logical forms of some NL sentences. If, however, LF is the logical form of some NL_i finite sentence, then, since the Constructor recursively enumerates all NL sentences, after a finite number of steps it will have constructed each NL_i sentence having LF as its logical form. The outputs of M for input LF are then determined in a finitary way, as indicated in the following pseudo-computer program.

Step 1: M receives LF. Step 2: the Constructor forms some finite NL sentence, say S_k. Step 3: M checks to see if the logical form of S_k is LF. This checking procedure is finitary, since LF and S_k are both finite. If the logical form of S_k is not LF, S_k is thrown away, and the device returns to Step 2. If it is, S_k is matched against $G(NL_i)$. Step 4. S_k either satisfies $G(NL_i)$ or it does not, that is, the statements of $G(NL_i)$ are either all true of S_k or not. Since S_k and $G(NL_i)$ are both finite, determination of this is also finitary. If S_k does not satisfy $G(NL_i)$, it is thrown away and the device returns to Step 2. If it does satisfy $G(NL_i)$, then S_k is an output of M for input LF. Since the Constructor provides a recursive enumeration of all finite NL sentences, after a finite number of steps, it will have constructed any NL_i sentence whose logical form is LF. Viewed in this way, M is a transducer in the sense that for any finite actual NL LF received as input, it will, after a finite number of steps, output each overall sentence well-formed in the NL defined by $G(NL_i)$ whose logical form is LF. To make M a realistic model, it would then be optimized by mechanisms which choose among the outputs so far defined.

It should be clear that an entirely parallel account can be given for M viewed as a parser. In that case, it takes a given phonetic representation PR as input, constructs NL sentences, checks to see if these have PR as their phonetic representation, and, if so, checks to see if they satisfy the grammar.

One important oversimplification in our account of the finitary operation of device M conceived as containing a non-constructive grammar deserves further comment. This relates to step 4, the determination of whether a constructed sentence satisfies $G(NL_i)$. It was claimed that this can be determined in a finitary way since both the grammar and the constructed sentence are finite.

However, this claim ignores the fact, specified in the account of non-constructive grammars in section 5.2, that grammars can contain corpus rules. To determine satisfaction for these involves more than checking any single sentence. For example, as discussed in Johnson and Postal (1980), certain NLs may have corpus rules precluding ambiguity in certain cases. We refer here to the phenomenon indicated by Chomsky (1965: 126–7):

> Second, even richly inflected languages do not seem to tolerate reordering when it leads to ambiguity. Thus in a German sentence such as 'Die Mutter sieht die Tochter,' in which the inflections do not suffice to indicate grammatical function, it seems that the interpretation will invariably be that 'Die Mutter' is the Subject ...

If such constraints are formulated as corpus rules, then, as indicated in Johnson and Postal (1980: chapter 14), it seems that determination of well-formedness involves a comparison of certain sentences with others. Very informally, object ... subject word order is allowed only if the resulting surface form is not identical to a subject ... object surface form of a distinct sentence.

Clearly, our account of the operation of device M incorporating finitary reference to a non-constructive grammar cannot account for knowledge of word-order disambiguation facts like those just mentioned. To that extent, the account given of the origin of linguistic knowledge is not fully realistic. However, while interesting in itself, this limitation of our account of device M does not bear on the main argument to which our construction was addressed. For, obviously, if our account fails to yield a fully finitary account of knowledge of the cited facts, an internalized constructive grammar will fail to yield an account in the same way. Therefore, such facts cannot serve to justify the view that instantiated human knowledge of sentences requires internalization of a constructor rather than a non-constructive grammar.

Of course, we have described nothing which could serve as an actual model of either speaker or hearer, since we have specified no heuristics which would make actual parsing and actual production possible. But this is not our task. Our only interest here was to show that the constructivity which, by *hypothetical* assumption (3c), is necessary to account for a native speaker's direct intuitive knowledge of sentence S of NL_i need not be attributed exclusively to an internalized grammar of NL_i. Rather, instantiated knowledge of S can be attributed to an internalized overall constructive system containing the non-constructive grammar embedded in a device M which incorporates the Constructor. Of course, in one sense, M is then itself a generative grammar of the finite sentences of NL_i; but it achieves this status only via incorporation of the non-constructive conditions on sentencehood in $G(NL_i)$. One can say that a speaker can know in principle each finite member of the actual *megacollection* of sentences characterized by an internalized non-constructive grammar because an equally internal producer/parser provides a recursive enumeration of the countability infinite subcollection of finite sentences. Given this possibility, a claim that internalized grammars *must* be constructive to account for speaker's knowledge of sentences, that is, to satisfy (3c), could only be justified by an argument that the notion 'knowledge of sentences' is not reconstructible in the schematic way just indicated. No such argument has ever been given and we see no way in which one could be. The unsound inference from (3c) to (3d) simply ignores the fact that producers and parsers will themselves, given their very nature, provide recursive enumerations of any sentences of a fixed NL which humans can actually be said to know.[5] Given this, the claim that the grammar is embedded in such devices must *also* be constructive suffers from the flaw of lacking any justification for the then assumed redundancy.

The appeal to producers and parsers for an account of knowledge of sentences which we have just sketched seems realistic. For an individual to have knowledge of a particular sentence surely involves instantiating it in some way. A psychogrammar per se provides no such instantiation but, at best, 'simultaneous' knowledge in principle of all of the infinite collection of sentences. No psychogrammar alone can account for the fact that at a given moment a speaker has intuitive knowledge of some particular sentence. But, being transducers, producers and parsers will instantiate individual sentences. Given an input semantic representation, a producer can be thought of as constructing a spe-

---

[5] That is, know directly, form intuitions about. Of course, just as computers have size bounds, internalized parsers/producers would as well, although these could be inessential.

cific sentence, including a phonetic representation; similarly, given an input phonetic representation, a parser can be thought of as constructing a specific sentence, including a semantic representation. Viewed in this way, parsers and producers manifest precisely the individuation of individual sentences needed for instantiated knowledge of those sentences. Moreover, it is difficult to make sense of the notion of a speaker actually knowing (rather than merely knowing in principle) some particular sentence in the absence of an ability to either parse its phonetic representation when that is presented or an ability to produce its phonetic representation when provided its semantic representation. Hence, not only is there no argument that intuitive knowledge of sentences cannot be attributed to the triple ⟨grammar, producer, parser⟩, such an attribution seems entirely justified.

In the terms we have sketched, it is in principle impossible for speakers to have the kind of *direct* knowledge of transfinite sentences which their internal parser/producer makes possible for finite sentences. Thus, knowledge of such sentences must be based on reasoning from direct knowledge of finite sentences. This is an entirely reasonable and unsurprising result. Moreover, recall that, even under the assumptions of (3), a speaker's ability to gain direct knowledge of most finite sentences exists *only* in principle (see Miller and Chomsky (1963: 467)). Limitations of memory, computational space, etc., preclude the actual mental instantiation even of most finite sentences. Hence, in fact, knowledge of huge finite sentences like (1bii) can only be gained in the same way as knowledge of transfinite sentences like (1biii). Put differently, humans cannot actually form direct intuitions about most finite sentences just as they cannot about any transfinite ones. Knowledge of all such sentences must be indirect, based on reasoning, rather than on the direct formation of intuitions as in the case of mentally manipulable sentences like (1bi).

To return to the main theme, our goal has been to show that even if, contrary to our view and to what is argued in Katz (1981, 1983), one accepts the conceptual interpretation of linguistic reality, this offers no ontological warrant for rejecting the linguistic existence of transfinite sentences. Summing up the argument so far vis-à-vis conceptualism, we have reasoned as follows. One way that a psychological interpretation of NLs could yield an ontological escape from the NL Vastness Theorem would be via a claim that psychogrammars are *necessarily* constructive. Since the notion of a psychologically real (finite) non-constructive grammar is as such non-problematic, this view can apparently only be supported via the further stipulations that (i) grammars are psychogrammars; (ii) a psychogrammar describes knowledge of sentences, and (iii) stricture (ii) is only possible if the psychogrammar is constructive. Statements (i) and (ii) can be taken as the position characteristic of what we have called standard conceptualism. While we deny the conjunction of (i) and (ii), in particular, (i), our argument is consistent with acceptance of their conjunction, since (iii) has no known justification. Even if psychogrammars are non-constructive, they could provide constructive knowledge of individual (finite) sentences via their incorporation in constructive producers and parsers. Hence, even the view that one must provide a constructive account of speakers' knowledge of sentences offers no support for the doctrine that psychogrammars per se are constructive. That is, standard conceptualism contains no justification for its traditional claim that the grammars internalized by children are constructive grammars. Thus it offers no basis for rejecting the view that NLs contain sentences of infinite size, in principle beyond the purview of constructive grammars.

6.3   Performance conceptualism

There are other possible versions of the conceptualist position which might justify the exclusion of transfinite sentences from the realm of linguistic objects but they are even less plausible than that just considered. For instance, as E. Keenan has observed (personal communication), some might wish to claim that linguistics is concerned only with the characterization of actually performable/understandable sentences. Such a view, even if interpreted conceptually rather than nominalistically, would immediately entail that transfinite sentences lie beyond the bounds of proper linguistic characterization. That is, this view would say that a grammar must characterize the collection of sentences which are in fact capable of yielding direct instantiated knowledge. Hence it would limit interest to (2a, b) to the exclusion of both (2c, d), and, in general, would only be concerned with finite collections of sentences. Since, however, the collections would be very large, a conceptualist approach might naturally claim that the proper characterization of such collections was a (constructive) psychologically real grammar, limited to a finite output via the incorporation of certain size restrictions. These parameters would be (non-arbitrarily) determined by the actual memory, computational, etc. limits of the human organism. Since this view interprets the conceptualist account of linguistic ontology in terms of non-linguistic limitations of the human organism, we refer to it as *performance conceptualism.*

But, evidently, the arguments against performance conceptualism as an account of the limits of linguistic reality include those justifying the early Chomskyan distinction between competence and performance. In particular, this position offers no basis for the fact, stressed by Miller and Chomsky (1963), that the ability to produce/understand sentences is extendable without new *linguistic* information merely by increasing available computing space and/or memory, even externally (as with paper and pencil). This would be inexplicable if psychogrammars were themselves performance-bounded. Miller and Chomsky (1963: 457) put this nicely as follows:

> One must be careful not to obscure the fundamental difference between, on the one hand, a device M storing the rules G but having enough computing space to understand in the manner of G only a certain proper subset L′ of the set L of sentences generated by G and, on the other hand, a device M* designed specifically to understand only the sentences of L′ in the manner of G. The distinction is perfectly analogous to the distinction between a device F that contains the rules of arithmetic but has enough computing space to handle only a proper subset Σ' of the set Σ of arithmetical computations and a device F* that is designed to compute only Σ'. Thus, although identical in their behavior to F* and M*, F and M can improve their behavior without additional instruction if given memory aids, but F* and M* must be redesigned to extend the class of cases they can handle.

Moreover, the analogy with arithmetic brings out another flaw in the view that psychogrammars should be performance-bounded. For, clearly, the principles which actually determine the *linguistic* performance limitations of real humans also determine *non-linguistic* performance limitations, e.g. arithmetical limitations. If then the limitations on dealing with large sentences are incorporated into a linguistic account, an Occam's razor violation ensues, since these same limitations must also be incorporated in descriptions of *non*-linguistic systems. There is no more reason for incorporating performance bounds on grammars of NLs than there is for imposing them on Peano's postulates or other axiomatizations of computational systems human use.

Further, any attempt to build performance limitations into grammars to yield a finite NL runs into the problem that performance is not necessarily constant across speakers of the 'same' NL or even constant for one speaker. This objection to finitist assumptions about NLs was formulated by Bennett (1976: 277):

> If the tribe are much like us, though, there will be no clean cut-off points. Rather, each tribesman will move smoothly from sentences he can easily understand to ones he cannot understand at all, through a middle region of sentences he can understand when he is fresh but not when he is tired, or which he can understand when he has thought about them but not immediately upon hearing them. Furthermore, the line between intelligible and unintelligible, smudged as it is, will be differently placed for different tribesmen, depending upon intelligence, memory, attention-span, and so on. There is therefore no clear work to be done by any particular finitist rule for any operator. Any rule which allows everything the brightest tribesman can understand will be far too generous for the linguistic performances of the duller members of the tribe. We could adopt different rules for different tribesmen, but it is better to explain the behavioural facts by differences in general intellectual abilities, ...

We conclude that there is no possibility of obtaining a viable ontologically motivated rejection of transfinite sentences through an interpretation of the conceptualist position which limits the goal to the description of performable/understandable sentences.[6] Thus performance conceptualism, like standard conceptualism,

[6] Obviously, the claim that linguistics is not limited to performable sentences in no way suggests any disparagement of the actual study of linguistic performance.

provides no rational (justified) grounds for rejecting the interpretation of the proof of the NL Vastness Theorem as a demonstration of a fundamental truth about NLs.

6.4   Radical conceptualism

Section 2 considered the now widely accepted interpretation of linguistic reality, which was referred to as standard conceptualism. This was introduced by Chomsky more than twenty years ago and maintained, developed and promulgated with great success. Standard conceptualism claims that grammars characterize knowledge, but it interprets this claim in a way which is at least superficially consistent with the traditional linguistic view that grammars describe NLs. This is accomplished by saying that internalized grammars generate NLs and that a speaker with internalized grammar G knows the NL generated by G, that is, as we have seen, has in principle knowledge of each member of that NL. Section 2 observed that this traditional view offers no known basis for rejecting the existence of transfinite sentences or for excluding them from NLs. This follows since the standard conceptualist claim that internalized grammars not only give necessary and sufficient conditions for sentencehood, but *in addition* in principle actually construct each sentence, is not justified by any known considerations, in particular, not by the goal of explicating linguistic knowledge or its acquisition.

In the last few years, however, Chomsky (1980a, 1980b, 1981a, 1981b) has begun to expound a view of linguistic reality which, while still conceptualist, differs sharply from his earlier, standard conceptualist position. We refer to this newer view as *radical conceptualism*, suggesting by this terminology not only a contrast with his own previous views but also with what have hitherto been taken as relatively non-controversial assumptions. The distinction between standard conceptualism and radical conceptualism is none the less sharp despite the fact that Chomsky's recent writings have largely failed to point out the radical shift in assumptions underlying them. Our point will be that radical conceptualism also offers no grounds for excluding transfinite sentences from the domain of linguistics. The lack of such grounds follows from the fact that radical conceptualism is a totally inadequate conceptual framework; it cannot justify an exclusion of transfinite sentences because it cannot justify anything at all.

Before considering radical conceptualism directly, a few background comments are in order, intended to cover briefly questions dealt with in detail in Katz (1981, 1983). We make a fundamental distinction between NLs and knowledge of NLs. NLs are abstract (platonist) objects, while knowledge of NLs is a psychological, possibly biological, object. This distinction is merely a special case of the general distinction between X and knowledge of X. No one confuses Aristotle and knowledge of Aristotle, Ronald Reagan's social security number and knowledge of that social security number, etc. Correspondingly, an object like English is entirely different from knowledge of English. To see this, it suffices to recognize the (infinite) realm of NLs for which there is not now and never has been any knowledge at all, that is, those NLs never internalized by any sentient creatures; see below. In general, knowledge of X presupposes the existence of X, but not conversely. There is no knowledge of round squares because there are no round squares and, further, many things evidently exist about which there is (at least as yet) no knowledge. Under the platonist view, grammars and grammatical theory are concerned exclusively with NLs and say nothing *directly* about knowledge of NLs. Thus there is nothing odd in the platonist claim that grammatical theory characterizes a realm of NLs most of which have not been learned and most of which are unlearnable (see below).

The general outlines of the platonist position about NLs and its contrast with others are nicely summed up by Katz (1981: 8–9):

> We feel our language is more a part of us than it would seem to be on a Platonist conception of natural languages. The feeling is real enough, but there is a question of whether it is a language – English, French, etc. – about which we have that feeling or something else closely related to language and as yet not distinguished from it. Whatever it is that we have these feelings about is what we acquire in the process we call 'language learning'. Since in this process we do not acquire English itself but rather knowledge of English, what we feel to be a part of us, what we feel intimately related to, and what, in fact, depends on us is our *knowledge of a language*. There is a distinction between a speaker's knowledge of a

language and the language itself – what the knowledge is knowledge of.

In these terms, although the platonist and standard conceptualist views about linguistics and linguistic reality are crucially different, they need not be interpreted as differing over the *existence of NLs*, or of sentences. The standard conceptualist position can take (and has taken) these as real things, as seen in section 2. That is, standard conceptualism takes (internally represented) grammars, NLs and sentences to all be real entities, claiming that possession of the former underlies an individual's knowledge of the latter.

In contrast, though, consider Chomsky's (1980a: 143) claim: 'The basic elements we consider are sentences; the grammar generates mental representations of their form and meaning.' The conceptualist character of Chomsky's newer position is immediately apparent, from its appeal to notions like 'mental representations of form/meaning'. But taking the phrasing literally, a contrast with standard conceptualism also emerges. In the latter terms (see the quote from Chomsky (1977b: 81) in section 2), psychogrammars generate sentences, not mental representations. If *sentences* and *mental representations of sentences* are distinct things, a grammar which generates the latter clearly fails to generate the former, contrary to the standard conceptualist tradition of generative work which has always taken grammars to be devices which generate NLs, that is, collections (sets) of sentences.

It is unclear just what Chomsky means by 'mental representations of sentences'. The most specific remark we have found is that in Chomsky (1980a: 5):

> When I use such terms as 'mind,' 'mental representation,' 'mental computation,' and the like, I am keeping to the level of abstract characterization of the properties of certain physical mechanisms, as yet almost entirely unknown. There is no further ontological import to such references to mind or mental representations and acts.

But on any reasonable reading, failure to take sentences and mental representations of them as distinct would yield an instantiation of the basic X/knowledge of X or, equivalently, X/(mental) representation of X confusion. The same abstract system, e.g. some algorithm, can obviously be represented in many distinct ways in the same or different computer or organism. The representations may differ from each other in many important properties, but this will not mean that the algorithm, as opposed to its various implementations, is not invariant. In the same way, there can obviously exist various distinct representations of the same sentence, mental or not, so that characterizations of the representations must be distinct both from each other and from characterizations of the sentences represented. In short, taking the claim in the first Chomsky quote above literally, radical conceptualism would minimally have abandoned the goal of characterizing sentences in favor of a description of something entirely different.

The question arises whether the radical conceptualist takes the further step of denying the existence of sentences. Logically, there might appear to be two versions of this doctrine, one of which denies that there are sentences as distinct from mental representations of sentences, and the other of which accepts that there are sentences but is simply not concerned with saying anything about them. Radical conceptualism is as yet so poorly expounded as to have offered no explicit statement as to which position is intended. It emerges from the criticisms that follow, however, that the correct interpretation of radical conceptualism on this score is that it simply involves a confusion of sentence and representation of sentence.

A fundamental equivocation on the notion of grammar is inherent in the radical conceptualist position. A key feature of Chomsky's conceptualism has always been, and remains, postulation of an innate mechanism which characterizes the class of possible human grammars. Sometimes this is referred to as *universal grammar*, sometimes as the *language faculty*, sometimes as a *language organ*. Assume, for purposes of argument, the existence of such a mechanism, call it IS. Viewed historically, at any given point in time, say now, two sorts of grammars are characterized by IS. First, there are the grammars of *attested* NLs like English, those with speakers, those for which the universe actually contains some knowledge. Second, there are the grammars of NLs so far not learned by any humans ('possible NLs').[7] Suppose, counter-

---

[7] One characteristic of the realm of abstract (platonist) objects is that possible Xs are just Xs. A possible positive integer is just a positive integer. Hence it is generally pointless to speak of 'possible NLs', which are just NLs tout court. The only value of the complex phrasing is that it focuses attention on the fact that one is speaking of NLs not all of which have been learned.

factually, that it made sense to think of the grammar of an attested NL as a description of mental representations. This could at best be an accidental feature of that grammar, one not determined by IS. For, evidently, (even Chomsky would agree) the grammars characterized by IS far exceed those which actually form the basis of linguistic knowledge in the sense in which native speakers have knowledge of English. For example, there will in the future be attested NLs not previously instantiated in human history. Uncontroversially then, there are so far unattested but real NLs, those of which the universe (presumably) so far contains no knowledge, although such knowledge is possible. Hence there are grammars of these so far unlearned NLs. Put differently, then, consideration of the very mechanism IS which is central to Chomsky's conceptualism already indicates that there are two different notions of grammar involved. Let us refer to these as *grammar*$_1$ and *grammar*$_2$.

To be a grammar$_1$, it suffices to be a formal object characterized by IS. To be a grammar$_2$, something must, however, both be a grammar$_1$ and be directly represented in some creature, that is, be learned or developed. A grammar$_2$ is a psychogrammar but a grammar$_1$ is not. Thus, viewed from the point of view of psychological–biological structure, if Chomsky is correct, all humans have an innate system which characterizes grammars (that is, grammar$_1$ s) of Latin, Swahili, Oneida, etc. But clearly English speakers do not know these NLs or have mental representations of any of their sentences, etc. There is no sense in which a monolingual English speaker has a psychogrammar of Oneida, even if (s)he is assumed to possess an innate IS determining a grammar$_1$ of this NL.

But the difference between two formal objects, one of which is only a grammar$_1$ and the other of which is in addition a grammar$_2$, is a contingent fact of human history.[8] From the linguistic point of view, any such distinction is purely accidental and of no theoretical interest. No principles of linguistics can possibly characterize this difference, nor should one want them to. This is evident when one considers that there was no grammar$_2$ of

---

[8] More precisely, given that some grammar$_1$s cannot be learned, grammar$_2$s are a subset of the proper subset of grammar$_1$s which are small enough actually to develop/be represented in humans.

English five thousand years ago. Hence the aggregate of grammar$_2$s changes over time, like the monarchs of England, while the collection of grammar$_1$s is invariant. But, clearly, at best (see below), it could only make sense to speak of the linguistically inessential notion of grammar$_2$ as generating mental representations, if by this one minimally means something represented in real minds. Thus, at best, the claim that grammars generate mental representations could only be true of the sense of grammar which is distinct from that referenced when one speaks of the fundamental (to conceptualists) notion of a collection of grammars characterized by IS.

Consider a grammar$_1$, call it G_x, which is *not* a grammar$_2$, but which is learnable by humans, that is, which is a *potential* grammar$_2$. What does G_x generate? The answer cannot under any sensible assumptions be mental representations. Logic tells us that the outputs are either sentences or are not sentences. Nothing has ever been said in the conceptualist linguistic literature to indicate that the outputs of grammars are anything other than sentences or mental representations of sentences. Since grammar$_1$s like G_x which are not grammar$_2$s cannot generate mental representations, their outputs must be sentences. But recall that a grammar$_2$ *is* a grammar$_1$. A grammar$_1$ qualifies as a grammar$_2$ merely by developing in some child. It follows that grammar$_2$s must also generate sentences, not mental representations of sentences. Hence Chomsky's radical conceptualist claim that grammars generate mental representations of sentences turns out, on analysis, to be incoherent under a reading where 'sentence' and 'mental representation of sentence' designate distinct categories of object. Most of the grammars IS determines (that is, grammar$_1$s) are not internalized in any humans (that is, are not psychogrammars). Hence, even if it made sense to speak of internalized grammars as generating mental representations, this could at best be a feature of grammar$_2$s and thus an accident from the point of view of the real linguistic (on the conceptualist viewpoint) realm of grammar$_1$s characterized by the language organ. Moreover, it does not make sense to speak in this way, since internalized grammars are, according to Chomsky's invariant conceptualist assumptions, simply instances of grammars specified by IS. And these grammars must generate sentences.

Further, as indicated in section 5.4, and returned to later in this section, most NLs, even most NLs having finite grammars, are in fact unlearnable by humans, that is, are such that no knowledge of them of the sort existent for English is even *possible*. In other words, most NLs, even if they have grammar$_1$s, can not have psychogrammars. The claim that grammars generate mental representations of sentences thus clashes totally with the fact that there are, and can be, no mental representations corresponding to most NLs, namely, the unlearnable ones. Consequently, there is, in yet another way, no sense to the radical conceptualist claim that NL grammars inherently describe mental representations (of sentences).

While we have formulated these criticisms with reference to the radical conceptualist position, in large part they apply also to the standard conceptualist view, which claims that grammars characterize linguistic knowledge. Clearly, no such claim makes any literal sense with respect to unlearned NLs. Moreover, even a modification to a claim that the grammar$_1$s characterized by IS describe 'potential knowledge' is untenable in the face of unlearnable NLs, for which there is not even any potential human knowledge (of the sort in question). More generally, this comment reveals an inadequacy of any conceptualist position, that is, any view claiming that NL grammars inherently describe an actual psychological domain. Such a view is incompatible with the fact that there are NLs which have never been learned and which are unlearnable. On the other hand, one can easily make sense in platonist terms of the notion of the sentences of an NL never learned by any creatures. But any claim that grammars inherently describe a psychological domain makes this incoherent. Radical conceptualism simply worsens an already bad conceptualist situation by failing to notice the lack of correspondence between the notions *NL sentence* and *mentally represented NL sentence*, no matter what detailed sense is given to the latter.

Next, observe that even for an attested NL like English, the claim that a grammar, even a psychogrammar, generates mental representations immediately creates otherwise unnecessary fundamental problems. Evidently, either the standard or radical conceptualist must minimally assume that any actual human mind or brain is finite, and thus that its very nature limits the objects which are in fact representable therein, for trivial non-linguistic reasons. Consequently, if psychogrammars generate mental representations of sentences, and mental representations are, as the term suggests, things actually present in real minds, in something like the sense in which, say, data or computations are present in real computers, the radical conceptualist position claims that NL grammars have a finite output, one containing no representation of cardinality greater than some finite k. This is inconsistent not only with the traditional generative position but with claims in the very works where radical conceptualism is advocated that the domain of grammar is infinite (see Chomsky (1980a: 220–1; 1981b 4–5)). Under this interpretation, radical conceptualism is simply an extraordinarily badly formulated version of performance conceptualism, a performance conceptualism so confused that it has not even recognized that its own assumptions preclude application to an infinite domain. When this inconsistency is purged, the view still has to be rejected, merely for the reasons cited in section 3.

Suppose though that the radical conceptualist tries to retain the view that grammars characterize an infinite domain while also maintaining that this domain is one of mental representations. This must yield a curious notion of mental representation which is neither mental nor which involves any representation. Since most finite sentences contain more words than the number of atoms in any real brain, or, indeed, in the entire known universe, the idea of representations of these sentences cannot be tied to any physical or psychological reality at all. Recall Chomsky's (1980a: 5) reference to 'abstract characterization of the properties of certain physical mechanisms'. Obviously there is no sense to the idea of a physical mechanism corresponding to a sentence bigger than the known universe. But most sentences in even a countably infinite collection would be bigger than this.

Consequently, the attempt to maintain an infinite linguistic domain can only combine with the idea that a grammar generates mental representations through adoption of some 'idealization'. Under this, the mental representations in question would not refer to actual objects in actual minds, but to ideal objects in ideal minds. These ideal minds would, in general, be very large indeed; most would be too big to even fit in the physical universe, if this is finite. In fact, acceptance that the grammatical domain includes just a countable infinity of objects requires, under this 'idealization', appeal to a countably infinite collection of ideal minds with $\aleph_0$ as the least upper bound on mind size, so that there will be at least one ideal mind available big enough for each finite sentence.

Can one take such 'idealizations' seriously? Clearly not. From one point of view, they make exactly as little sense as an attempt to interpret Peano's postulates in terms of computers of unbounded size – that is, to claim that these postulates describe computer representations of integers – with the real limits of actual computers replaced by an 'idealization'. From another point of view, it is clearly deleterious for linguistics to posit *two* infinite realms, one consisting of mental representations which are not actually mental and not actually representations and the other consisting of ideal minds most of which are bigger than the universe, rather than to simply recognize, as in platonist terms, a single infinite realm of sentences.

A traditional objection to platonism is that it requires epistemologically unwanted appeal to abstractions too remote from experience. Chomsky's conceptualism might seem to offer a haven from this, with its apparent comforting appeal to aspects of at least potentially examinable mind/brains. Unfortunately, one sees that, instead, the apparent psychological concreteness of mental representations offered in radical conceptualist terms is entirely illusory. Instead of something concrete or epistemologically palpable, one is immediately led to two unobservable, non-palpable infinite realms of abstractions. These differ from the platonist's realm of sentences (abstract objects) in no way epistemologically but chiefly in (i) their lack of clarity and (ii) their excrescence. By the latter we mean that all reference to ideal minds in linguistics is totally unmotivated except by the radical conceptualist view that grammars specify mental representations. There is no possible reason for basing grammatical study on assumptions like those offered by radical conceptualism.

Viewed in another way, the claim that grammars generate mental representations of sentences rather than sentences might be taken as a straightforward confusion of a grammar per se with the device M of section 2, that is, as a confusion of a grammar with a parser/producer. Since, as already noted, Chomsky's earlier standard conceptualist writings had clearly and properly distinguished these, both the distinctiveness of radical conceptualism and its clear relative inferiority to standard conceptualism are again evident. The interpretation of radical conceptualism as confusing grammars with parser/producers seems proper since, by their very nature, internalized devices functioning as parsers/producers would yield objects that could reasonably be called mental representations. The fact that minds are finite then entails that most sentences cannot be parsed or produced; but this is unparadoxical, since, of course, even most finite sentences cannot in fact be produced or parsed by humans or even Woocoos.

We have considered two interpretations of Chomsky's inchoate radical conceptualist claim that NL grammars generate mental representations of sentences. One interpretation takes the terminology literally, and leads immediately to the conclusion that grammars have a finite range of objects small enough to actually 'fit' in real human mind/brains. This view offers a principled grounds for rejecting the linguistic existence of transfinite sentences, but only at the cost of also rejecting almost all finite sentences. Moreover, this first interpretation is inconsistent with both past conceptualist claims and current radical conceptualist ones, which stress that the grammatical system is infinite. Hence, as such, the first interpretation fails the most minimal constraints on an intellectual system. Even if made consistent by rejecting the view that there is an infinite domain, this interpretation reduces radical conceptualism to performance conceptualism; it must then be rejected on the general grounds which undermine the latter, many of them first given by Chomsky himself in arguing for the performance/competence distinction. This first interpretation of talk of mental representations thus certainly provides no grounds at all for excluding transfinite sentences from the domain of linguistics.

On a second interpretation, the mental representations specified by a radical conceptualist grammar are not actual objects in real mind/brains but ideal objects found in ideal minds, most of which are bigger than the known universe. This conception is superior to the first being consistent, but requires recognition of otherwise useless and unmotivated infinite realm of ideal minds. Hence it is immediately inferior to the elemental platonist view that NLs involve one infinite realm of sentences. Consequently, Occam's razor precludes adoption of the factually excrescent world of ideal minds. While this suffices to show that the second interpretation of 'mental representations' offers no justified grounds for excluding transfinite sentences, it is perhaps worth observing that we see no difference in principle between appealing to huge finite ideal minds to represent huge finite sentences and appealing to transfinite ideal minds to represent transfinite sentences. That is, even in its own terms, appeal to ideal minds offers no clear basis for excluding transfinite sentences.

Moreover, if the notion of transfinite mind seems silly, the essential silliness inheres in the idea that one needs to posit minds as big as the (linguistic) objects one recognizes. If radical conceptualism truly assumes this, then it already needs infinite minds independent of linguistics, to deal with the infinite non-linguistic collections of mathematics and logic. Otherwise, as stressed in Katz (1981) throughout, the conceptualist is in the position of making a never-justified distinction between the realm of mathematico-logical objects and the realm of linguistic objects. Neither standard nor radical conceptualism has offered the slightest grounds for believing that infinite collections can be recognized in mathematics without infinite minds but that the parallel assumption is not possible in linguistics. It seems that at the best a consistent homogenous radical conceptualism should adopt some form of *intuitionist* view of mathematics and logic and *minimally* reject any collections beyond the countably infinite; see Fraenkel, Bar-Hiller and Levy (1973: chapter 4). But it would not be enough to simply adopt such a view; it would also be necessary to justify it. We conclude that talk of grammars generating 'mental representations' cannot and should not be taken seriously and provides not the slightest barrier to the recognition of transfinite sentences in NLs.

There is a final aspect to Chomsky's radical conceptualist view that grammars generate mental representations. Interpret this as a claim about the grammars which Chomsky himself proposes. Then it is readily apparent in another way that the claim makes no sense. For the actual generative devices Chomsky appeals to in the works introducing his radical conceptualist philosophy are of the same general nature as those he has previously appealed to: phrase structure rules, lexical rules, transformations, etc. These devices generate strings of symbols, or trees, or sequences of trees, etc. Nothing in the slightest about these objects is mental. Hence, with respect to Chomsky's own grammatical proposals, the claim that grammars generate mental representations must be either (i) false; (ii) vacuous, that is, merely an empty, pseudo-psychological way of saying they generate sentences (strings, (sequences of) trees, etc.), or else (iii) Chomsky's proposed grammar fragments must be on these grounds alone wrong reconstructions of psychogrammars which, by his assumption, generate mental representations and thus not strings, trees, etc.

Recapitulating so far, the initial idea defining radical conceptualism is that grammars generate mental representations of sentences, not sentences themselves. But since there is no way to interpret this claim so as to provide a coherent or sensible framework, radical conceptualism is from the outset untenable.

Next, radical conceptualism is characterized by an extraordinary view of the relation between grammars and NLs. To see this, consider Chomsky's reply (1980a: 123–8) to a claim by Hintikka (1977) that certain properties of the English expression *any* render the collection of English sentences non-recursively enumerable. We need not consider Hintikka's argument itself. Chomsky (1980a: 126) says:

> Hintikka maintains that the argument is 'a clear cut counter-example to generative grammar.' If the argument were valid, it might be a counter-example to the belief that a generative grammar, represented in the mind, determines the set of well-formed sentences. It in no way impugns the belief that a generative grammar is represented in the mind, but rather implies that this grammar does not in itself determine the class of what we might choose to call 'grammatical sentences'; rather, these sentences are the ones that meet both some condition that involves the grammar and a condition lacking a decision procedure.

The first point to be made about this position is that it shows Chomsky cannot now consistently adopt the view, criticized in section 2, that knowledge of sentences depends on possessing an internalized grammar which actually constructs those sentences. In the quoted passage, Chomsky is in effect granting that speakers can know a collection of sentences *despite* lacking a device which recursively enumerates them. In short, radical conceptualism cannot justify the positing of internalized *generative* grammars on the grounds that these are necessary for linguistic knowledge.

The second comment which Chomsky's reaction to Hintikka's

argument engenders is that a grammar is by definition a system specifying the necessary and sufficient conditions for membership in some collection of objects. Hence, again by definition, there can be no grammar of an NL M if there is no NL M. The standard way of showing that some proposed NL grammar is incorrect is to show that it fails to accord with the bounds of that NL: saying something is a sentence which is not or failing to say something is a sentence which is. Notably, Chomsky gives no grounds for not taking Hintikka's putative result in precisely this way, that is, as a refutation of the claim that NL grammars have the property (defining a recursively enumerable set) which Chomsky had, in his standard conceptualist stance, always assumed they had.

Instead of drawing such a conclusion, Chomsky (1980a: 126–7) continues:

> Human languages might accord with these conclusions [Hintikka's] and perhaps even do. It will still be proper to say that the fundamental cognitive relation is 'knowing a grammar,' but we will now conclude that a grammar does not in itself define a language (not an unreasonable conclusion in any event, for reasons already mentioned), and that in fact languages may not be recursively definable, even though the conditions that they meet are represented in the mind, hence brain. In this case, various questions would remain to be settled as to what we would choose to call 'a language,' but they do not seem to be particularly interesting, because the notion 'language' itself is derivative and relatively unimportant. We might even dispense with it, with little loss.

Such radical conceptualist comments are far removed from Chomsky's (1957: 13) earlier view: 'The grammar of L will thus be a device that generates all of the grammatical sequences of L and none of the ungrammatical ones.' The contrast thus illustrates strikingly the distance between radical conceptualism and distinct positions, including Chomsky's own earlier views.

Not only is this aspect of the radical conceptualist position different, it is completely unjustified. If there are no NLs, there can be no notion of their *correct* grammars. Thus anything at all could be called a grammar and NL grammars would have ceased to play any role in the characterization of a factual domain. Chomsky's claim that postulation of an internalized generative grammar is not falsified by showing that the grammar fails to accord with the boundaries of an NL largely eliminates any requirement of accountability for the postulated grammar. If it is a factual hypothesis that some individual has internally represented a *constructive* grammar, then a demonstration that the linguistic domain that grammar supposedly characterized is not a recursively enumerable set falsifies that claim.

Further, a real grammar cannot, by definition, fail to define an NL, namely, just that collection it characterizes. Hence, if there are real NL grammars, there are necessarily real NLs. If then a linguist presents a grammar, G, as a characterization of some NL, L, and G fails to specify exactly L, the only conclusion is that G is an incorrect account of any real grammar of L. Is it not curious that Chomsky should have proposed such an extreme methodological position without attempting to show why, for example, it could not be used in ways even he must find intolerable? For instance, in the late 1950s Chomsky presented arguments showing that purely finite state and phrase structure grammars were inadequate. But, following his current methodology, the finite state or phrase structure partisan need merely have replied: the arguments against finite state/phrase structure grammars do not impugn the belief that a finite state/phrase structure grammar is represented in the mind but rather imply that this grammar does not in itself determine the class of what we might choose to call 'grammatical sentences'. Hence on his own current radical conceptualist principles, none of Chomsky's arguments justified his adoption of transformational grammar as an account of internalized grammars.

A third basic notion of Chomsky's recent radical conceptualist view is the unargued intimation that NLs are not real, although grammars are. This position was already seen in the second of the two quotes above from Chomsky (1980a) concerning Hintikka's argument and is stated even more starkly in Chomsky (1981b: 5):

Pursuing these questions, we shift our focus from the language to the grammar represented in the mind/brain. The language now becomes an epiphenomenon: it is whatever is characterized by the rules of the grammar (perhaps, in conjunction with other systems of mind, or even other factors ...). The grammar in a person's mind/brain is real; it is one of the real things in the world. The language (whatever that may be) is not.

One is struck by the remoteness of this position from works like Chomsky (1957) and by the absence of any argument for the asserted non-reality of NLs. What is at work is apparently a crude physicalism. Grammars are supposed to be actually physically present in mind/brains, taken as physical objects and presumably to partake of their reality. But, since NLs are obviously not physical, Chomsky takes them as not real. These positions suggest that in considerable part Chomsky's current radical conceptualism not only contains important features of performance conceptualism but elements which are nothing short of nominalistic. It is perhaps well to recall that his earliest theoretical work (Chomsky (1955)) was frankly nominalistic although, as Katz (1981: 33–4; 43) observes, certain modifications in the published version (Chomsky (1975)) obscure this point. In any event, the relevant claims are completely inadequate.

First, they ignore the distinction between grammar$_1$ and grammar$_2$. Clearly, grammar$_1$s can not be assumed to be physically represented in the same sense that grammar$_2$s are, and if it were the physical representation of the latter that made them real, then grammar$_1$s would be unreal, and IS, that is, Chomsky's postulated language organ, would characterize a collection including unreal objects. Second, as already noted, since most NLs have never been learned, no grammar$_2$ of them is actually represented in any brain. The radical conceptualist might then retreat to the claim that grammars are real because they are *representable*, rather than actually represented. But, presumably, storage space issues aside, any finite, formally stateable system is representable. So mere representability does not pick out NL grammars from among all possible representable systems, which it is clearly not Chomsky's intention to award the reality of NL grammars. Moreover, in the case of unlearnable NLs, no psychogrammar is even potentially representable.

Returning to Chomsky's persistent view that there is an innate linguistic schematism which characterizes the grammars of NLs, one can ask whether such assumptions yield a coherent, tenable view that representable grammars are real although the NLs they describe are not. In particular, one can consider the idea that NL grammars might be real only because they are *both* representable and defined by such a system. Representable systems not defined in this way might then tenably not be real. Let us refer to any system characterizing a collection of NL grammars as SY, putting temporarily aside the question whether SY is biologically innate in fixed classes of creatures.

Consider the relation between the hypothesized SY and the collection of grammars it determines, in particular, the *number* of grammars that have to be specified by SY. Chomsky (1981c: 277) claims that: '... the theory of transformational grammar (t.g.) that I have been investigating for about the past 10 years permits only a finite number of grammars in principle; ...' Gazdar (1981b: 283) correctly observes that this claim of Chomsky's is completely without support since no proof is cited and the notions necessary to any such proof, e.g. 'longest possible base rule', 'longest possible lexical entry', 'longest possible filter', etc., remain undefined. Pullum (1983) shows in great detail that not only is no proof given, but none is possible. Irrespective of whether any theory actually has the consequence Chomsky claimed, one can easily see that a genuine theorem showing that some theory determines only a finite number of NL grammars would be a proof that that theory is a false account of NLs.[9] That is, if, as is terminologically sensible and consistent with recent tradition, grammars specify lexical properties, it is straightforward to show that there are an infinite number of NL grammars. This will follow from the fact that there are infinitely many *finitely specifiable* NLs.

That the number of NLs is infinite follows from purely lexical considerations. For the lexical characteristics of an NL involve, minimally, the collection of phoneme strings associated with (partially defining) the morphemes of that NL. Suppose SY makes

---

[9] Gazdar (1981b: 283) claims that Chomsky's assertion that there are only finitely many NL grammars is unfalsifiable. He reaches this conclusion from the consideration that any claim that the ith parameter of grammars has the maximum value k can only be falsified by finding an NL whose best grammar requires the value $k + 1$ for the ith parameter. But Gazdar's assumption is too narrow and incorrect. Were it correct, it would be equally impossible for the same reason to falsify a claim that the longest sentence in any NL is k words long (k finite). Gazdar's conclusion ignores the possibility that one can show that the best grammar imposes no upper bound on k at all, a conclusion derivable in many cases with no appeal to actual observations justifying a greater value than k, as shown by the arguments in chapter 3.

available a non-null set, P, of universal phonemes, say in terms of features as in Chomsky and Halle (1968: 335). There is then good reason to assume that a *minimum* bound on the number of distinct NLs is given by the cardinal number Q, specified as in (4):

(4) $Q = \#X$, where X is the collection of distinct sets of strings over P.

The determination of magnitude in (4) is justified as follows.

(5)   a.   The set of distinct lexical items can be no smaller than the set of all possible phonological morphemes.

   b.   The logic of chapter 3 shows that there is no length bound, finite or transfinite, on the morphophonemic representations of morphemes.

   c.   But let us ignore this and consider only *finite* morphemes and, further, also artificially restrict attention to only *finite* sets of morphemes.

   d.   It then follows that the value of Q in (4) is at least equivalent to the number of distinct finite sets of all finite strings over the elements of P.[10]

   e.   Regardless of the cardinality of P, in the absence of a *specific finite* bound on the length of morphemes,[11] the number of distinct strings over P is $\aleph_0$.

   f.   The value of Q in (4), the number of distinct finite 'lexicons' over P, is then given by a fundamental set-theoretical principle (see Eisenberg (1971: 241)) which says that the set of all finite subsets of a denumerable set is denumerable, i.e. of the order $\aleph_0$.

[10] One can object that this set includes many subsets which are not plausible 'lexicons', e.g. those containing only a single string, etc. But even granting that these are not possible 'lexicons' does not affect the cardinality of X in (4), since the set of such 'strange' morpheme collections is finite and subtracting any finite number of elements from an infinite set leaves a set with the same cardinality as the original.

[11] Notably, actual works on phonology, e.g. Chomsky and Halle (1968), not only specify no bound on morpheme length but do not suggest there is one.

Hence, even artificially limiting NLs to 'lexicons' consisting of only finitely many finite phonological representations of morphemes, there are $\aleph_0$ 'lexicons', hence at least $\aleph_0$ distinct NLs. This inference could only fail if there were some universal laws of phoneme combination, distinct from length laws, which somehow restricted the possible combinations of phonemes in such a way as to leave only a finite set of universally 'legal' morphophonemic representations. No such laws have ever been proposed, nor is there any basis for believing there are any. Consequently, the calculation in (5) appears unproblematic.

It follows that SY must characterize at least $\aleph_0$ grammars *if* it can be shown that at least this many NLs have grammars. One cannot only show this but the much stronger point that at least $\aleph_0$ NLs have *finite* grammars. To do this, isolate the 'lexicon' from the rest of NL structure by restricting attention to an NL which is identical to an attested NL, say English, except lexically. Assume then that there is at least one finite grammar of English. This must contain, inter alia, a number of specifications about morphemes, e.g. one indicating that $\langle fear \rangle$, say as a Noun, is associated with a meaning involving reference to a certain kind of emotion. Make only the minimal assumption that this aspect of the grammar is a pairing of the phonological form of the morpheme with some finite meaning structure we can call M. Hence this aspect of the grammar of English reduces in effect to the ordered pair:

(6) $(\langle fear \rangle, M)$

Recognition that (6) is part of a real finite grammar of English combines with the fact that there are indefinitely many universally possible finite morphemes to determine that there are infinitely many finite NL grammars.

One need only consider grammars *entirely identical* to that of English except that the representation $\langle fear \rangle$ in (6) is replaced by the representation of some distinct finite morpheme. Given that there are $\aleph_0$ distinct finite morphemes, the collection of all and only the grammars specified starting from the grammar of English and replacing $\langle fear \rangle$ in (6) by the representation of some universally possible morpheme is a set of grammars all distinct from the original and from each other and having $\aleph_0$ elements. To make the relation between the 'new' grammars and the original even stricter, one can assume that the 'new' morphemes are constructed not from random members of the universal set of phonemes P, but only from the proper subset of this found in actual English morphemes. No limitation on the cardinality of grammars arises even if one insists further that all the phoneme combinations in this set of 'new' morphemes obey all of the actual phonotactic constraints obeyed by attested English morphemes. Hence, the conclusion that there are infinitely many finite grammars of NLs follows from the existence of infinitely many distinct phonological morphemes plus the axiomatic assumption that there is one finite grammar.

The consequence could only fail to follow if SY contained some laws of grammarhood sensitive to phonological shape. That is, there would have to be sound symbolism laws precluding certain combinations of phonemes from being associated with the meaning representation M in (6). Moreover, these laws would have to be such that only a finite number of phonological morphemes could be associated with any fixed element such as M. Nothing suggests the existence of any such laws, which have never been proposed in any sketch of grammatical theory. Given this, there is no reasonable way to deny that each of the new distinct finite grammars whose construction we have sketched is the grammar of some NL. Consequently, the conclusion from (5) that there are at least $\aleph_0$ finite NL grammars is extremely well supported. However, this demonstration is totally incompatible with the currently common view that a grammatical theory should characterize exactly that collection of NLs learnable by humans. We return to this point at the end of the present section.

We have argued for the claim that there are at least $\aleph_0$ NLs and $\aleph_0$ finite NL grammars because this result reveals in a new way why Chomsky's unsupported radical conceptualist view that there could be real grammars without real NLs cannot be taken seriously. Surely, a minimal condition on any theory T, of NL grammars is:

(7)   T determines at least one finite grammar for each NL having at least one finite grammar.

Recall, for instance, Chomsky's (1965: 24) specification: 'We may, correspondingly, say that *a linguistic theory is descriptively adequate* if it makes a descriptively adequate grammar available for each natural language.' Since there are at least $\aleph_0$ distinct finite

NL grammars, if SY is even potentially a correct account of NLs, it must specify no less than $\aleph_0$ grammars. The relation between SY and the collection of grammars it specifies is then of essentially the same logical character as the relation between an individual grammar and the (megacollection of) sentences it specifies. If, as Chomsky's radical conceptualist position asserts, a real grammar could fail to specify a real NL, then, by a parity of reasoning, a real SY could fail to specify a real collection of grammars. Assume this for argument. Either there is a real collection of grammars or there is not. If the latter, SY is totally unmotivated as an object of scientific relevance. Linguistics hardly needs a complex schematism (posited as innate in humans or not) to characterize a *nonexistent* collection. If, however, there is a real collection of grammars, and, on radical conceptualist conceptions, SY fails to characterize this real collection, one can only conclude that SY is false and the conceptions in question are incorrect. Moreover, since the argument based on (5) shows that there is a real (in fact, infinite) collection of NL grammars, the view that SY fails to characterize this real collection of NL grammars obviously just indicates that SY is not a proper scientific account of this aspect of reality.

Now, consider a theory, T, of NLs and their grammars which is, by hypothesis, *correct.* Minimally then, T characterizes an infinite collection, CG, of grammars. Suppose further, following Chomsky, that there truly is a system, call it again IS, innate in human beings which characterizes a collection, IG, of NL grammars. Clearly, it is *logically* possible that IG $\neq$ CG, that is, IS might, for example, not characterize the set of all finite grammars for all NLs having finite grammars. This would mean that humans are innately equipped with a system which, if interpreted as a theory of NLs or NL grammars, is a *false* theory of these objects, in something like the way in which various calculators are inherently equipped with limitations which, in effect, make them false theories of the class of arithmetical computations (see Katz (1981: 224–5) for related discussion). For the (platonist) linguist, whose goal is to characterize NLs and not human nature, no problem arises. T is uncompromisingly chosen as the proper grammatical theory, and one concludes, as in the preceding sentences, that human nature involves a (partially) false innate theory, IS $\neq$ T. For the person whose interest is in human nature and not in NLs, the conclusion is also clear. The false theory of NLs is justifiably picked as the system to be characterized. No problem arises as long as the psychologically oriented investigator does *not* claim that IS = T. Completely unjustifiable, however, is any attempt to infer from the *mere* innateness of IS the view that it is *thereby* the correct theory of NLs.

To see the impossibility of such an inference, note that it is logically possible that distinct (classes of) creatures might have distinct innate grammar defining systems. Suppose, for instance, that it turned out that human males and females had (slightly) distinct innate systems, one having some property P and the other not having it. Then this logical possibility would combine with a projection from innateness to correctness as a theory of NLs to yield the conclusion that the correct theory of NLs is one *both* having and not having property P. But consistency is the minimal condition to be met by any true theory.

The property P just cited might be one which would make it impossible to learn ('in the ordinary way') some NL, L_x. We are often told that humans can learn any NL if presented with samples in the usual way (see the quote from Wexler, Culicover and Hamburger (1975) below). But there is no real assurance that this is the case. It might be that the NLs which are unlearnable by e.g. men, but are learnable by women just have so far not been learned by any community of women.

It follows that even the *demonstrated* innateness of a system defining grammars of NLs would provide no basis for the correct-ness of that system as a theory of NLs. Evidently, the innateness of one or another grammar-defining system is entirely irrelevant to the determination of the correct theory of NLs. Another way to see this is to observe that the view that there is an innate grammar-defining system is, regardless of its plausibility or truth, *logically contingent*. But surely the logical alternative that there is no *innate* grammar-defining system no more entails the conse-quence that there is no correct theory of NLs and their grammars than the alternative that there might be no *innate* number-defining system entails the consequence that there is no correct theory of numbers. This indicates that the biological innateness of a grammar-defining system has no more to do with the nature of NLs than the various built-in constraints on computer computa-tion have to do with the nature of numbers.

Our argument that an innate grammar-defining system is irrelevant to a true theory of grammars and NLs shares much of its logic with an argument given by Chomsky (1980a: 251–2) about scientific theories:

> It is conceivable that we might discover the principles that underlie the construction of intelligible theories, thus arriving at a kind of 'universal grammar' of scientific theories. And by analyzing these principles, we might determine certain properties of the class of accessible theories. We might then raise the following question: What is the relation between the class of humanly accessible theories and the class of true theories? It is possible that the intersection of these classes is quite small, that few true theories are accessible.

The key notion advanced by Chomsky here is that accessible (humanly knowable) theories and true theories are logically distinct categories. It follows that in any domain, hence a fortiori in the linguistic domain, a psychologically real theory might be false and the true theory might fail to be psychologically real or accessible. The fact that a psychologically real theory develops because of some innate mechanism obviously then does nothing to guarantee the truth of that theory. It is, for example, logically possible that some creatures somewhere have a nature which determines an innate theory equivalent to Newtonian physics or phlogiston theory. The existence of these creatures would lend no support to those (false) physical theories. And, for the same reasons, if humans do have some innate system of grammar characterization, this can lend no support to any theory consistent with that system nor can it disconfirm any theory inconsistent with it.

We have been discussing the radical conceptualist idea that grammars are real but NLs are not real. The discussion has proceeded from Chomsky's actual discussion of represented grammars to representable grammars and then to representable grammars specified by some system SY. At no point has there appeared any sensible, still less tenable, interpretation for a claim that grammars could be real but NLs not. In particular, there is no way to derive this from the putative physical representation of grammars (which is false even for most finite NL grammars) or the hypothesized physical representation of SY, which still relates to most NL grammars just as a physically represented grammar relates to sentences and which is irrelevant to the true character-ization of NLs.

We have shown that most grammars have never been repre-sented and thus that their reality cannot depend on physical rep-resentation, nor on the physical representation of an innate system defining them. Consider again, though, that relatively small set of grammars which, as a result of historical accidents,[12] are or have been physically represented. Even these, the grammar$_2$s (psychogrammars) of our earlier remarks, cannot sensibly be said to have gained any *physical* reality via such representation, con-trary to what Chomsky's recent remarks seem to imply (see the quote above from Chomsky (1980a: 5) with its reference to physi-cal mechanisms). Even given that a particular grammar is physi-cally represented in some brain, that grammar can still not be *identified* with anything physical. A grammar as an intensional object, rather than merely as some piece of physically instantiated formalism, only exists given an *interpretation* of the formalism, which can never be physical. This is as obvious as the fact that the actual physical states of a computer are only associated with some program and hence, derivatively, with the algorithm the program represents via a non-physical interpretation. Or, as expressed by Slezak (1982: 43):

> Indeed, to speak of a Turing machine as performing 'compu-tations' as we generally do, is already to have taken a step away from what is, strictly speaking, the actual behavior of the machine: a 'tape expression' for a Turing machine con-sisting of symbols in its alphabet is intrinsically no different from any other component of the machine; its special staus derives from the fact that we associate our numerals with the tape expressions, and we are then able to regard the oper-ations of the machine as calculations on numbers.'

An essentially analogous point is made by Putnam (1975b: 293):

> Assume that one thesis of materialism (I shall call it the 'first thesis') is correct, and we are, as wholes, just material systems obeying physical laws. Then the second thesis of classical materialism cannot be correct – namely, our mental states,

[12] That is, accidents from the point of view of any theory of NL grammars.

e.g. *thinking about next summer's vacation*, cannot be *identical* with any physical or chemical states. For it is clear from what we already know about computers, etc., that whatever the program of the brain may be, it must be physically possible, though not necessarily feasible, to produce something with that same program but quite a different physical and chemical composition. Then to identify the state in question with its physical or chemical realization would be quite absurd, given that that realization is in a sense quite accidental, from the point of view of psychology ...

Evidently then, the fact that some grammars are somehow represented physically does nothing to make them physical and non-abstract any more than the fact that some sorting algorithm is represented in a computer serves to make that sorting algorithm a physical object. Similarly, chiseling a representation of the NL Vastness Theorem into a rock will not convert that theorem into a physical object. No attempt to attribute *physical* reality to grammars can thus ever succeed.

In the other direction, there is no way the unchallenged *nonphysical* nature of NLs can support Chomsky's view that they are not real. This could at best only be a viable justification if one was, inter alia, ready to reject all abstractions ... numbers, sets, propositions, symphonies, theorems, the law of contradiction, etc. But since such abstractions underly all of even Chomsky's linguistic theorizing, no such interpretation is possible. Consequently, even for Chomsky, the abstract (platonist) character of NLs offers no basis for denying them reality. No other reasons are given. Combined with the fact that real grammars necessarily determine real NLs, we can find no grounds whatever in Chomsky's recent radical conceptualist remarks for the view that NLs are not real.

There is another argument against the claim that NLs are unreal. Consider how this idea interacts with Chomsky's claim about an innate linguistic organ. As Katz (1981) observes, what sense could there be to the notion of a *linguistic* organ if there are no NLs? Clearly, the identification of some aspect of mind as in particular a *linguistic* aspect depends on being able to correlate the functions of that aspect with something which is (i) external to it and (ii) linguistic. One could hardly claim to have discovered an aspect of mind which provides knowledge of numbers if there were no numbers. Hence, for the notion of a linguistic organ to have content, there must be NLs. Chomsky seems to have thus currently adopted a stance rather parallel to that of a psychologist who denies there is extrasensory perception but simultaneously asserts that there is a mental organ underlying human competence in the extrasensory domain. Since skepticism about NLs is incompatible with Chomsky's linguistic nativism and his radical conceptualist position involves both, it again appears to even lack consistency.

There is one final remark to be made about the radical conceptualist claim that NLs are not real. For Chomsky, both individual grammars and each sentence they describe are, and always have been, taken to be finite. If, therefore, there are no NLs, there is absolutely no aspect of linguistic reality which could be infinite. Yet, again inconsistently, Chomsky (1981b: 4) continues to speak of the linguistic domain as infinite.

We mentioned earlier that the demonstration that there are an infinitude of finite NL grammars is incompatible with the currently common doctrine that all NLs are learnable by human beings. Since this conflict reveals sharply the difference between characterizing NLs and characterizing some psychological/ biological reality, it is worth considering in slightly greater detail.

The view we are rejecting is representable as:

(8)   The collection of (finite) NL grammars is identical to the collection of NL grammars learnable by human beings (in the ordinary way).

The doctrine in question is seen in such statements as the following from Wexler, Culicover and Hamburger (1975: 218):[13]

A theory of (first) language acquisition defines a procedure which models the essential characteristics of how the child acquires his language. This procedure must be powerful enough to learn any natural language, since we start with the fundamental observation that any normal child can learn any natural language, given the proper environment.

---

[13] More recently, Wexler (1982: 93) contemplates the view that the class of NL grammars and the class of learnable NL grammars might be distinct.

The same view is seen in the claim by Osherson and Weinstein (1982: 78):

> A defining feature of natural languages is that precisely the natural languages can be learned by normal human infants in the ordinary way. Consequently, one condition on a theory of natural language is that it specify a class of languages that are learnable in this sense.

Finally, the same idea appears in Chomsky (1977a: 12–13):

> Each grammar is a theory of a particular language, specifying formal and semantic properties of an infinite array of sentences. These sentences, each with its particular structure, constitute the language generated by the grammar.[14] The languages so generated are those that can be 'learned' in the normal way.

In fact, the equivalence in (8) is entailed by the standard conceptualist view that an NL grammar is a description of linguistic competence (= linguistic knowledge). For, obviously, if an NL is unlearnable, it cannot be learned, hence has not been, and never will be, learned. There is no *actual* competence anywhere corresponding to the grammar (grammar$_1$) of an unlearned NL and there is not even any *potential* competence corresponding to the grammar$_1$ of an unlearnable NL. So it could at best make sense to say that it was an essential property of NL grammars (even grammar$_1$s) to characterize competence or even potential competence only if every NL grammar were learnable.

But the demonstration that there are an infinite number of finitely specifiable NL grammars is in effect a proof that there are unlearnable NLs, if by learnable one means actually representable in a real human being ('learnable in the ordinary way by an ordinary human child'). This again follows from nothing more than the existence of some finite bound or range of finite bounds on human memory capacity. For evidently the infinite set of pos-

---

[14] This hardly very old passage of course states a position inconsistent with Chomsky's more recent claim that NLs are not real. This quote, representing what we have called standard conceptualism, highlights the point that nowhere has Chomsky suggested how there can be (i) real grammars, (ii) real sentences, but (iii) nonetheless, not real NLs.

sible finite 'lexicons' of finite morphemes includes infinitely many
with e.g. more elements than the number of electrons in the
known universe and infinitely many with individual lexical items
of a size greater than is humanly storable. Hence storage limitation considerations alone suffice to show that many, in fact,
most, finitely specifiable NL grammars are not in fact learnable by
real human beings. Thus, even if it made sense to say that the
grammars of attested NLs describe competence or any psychological object at all, this notion collapses in the face of the fact
that most finite NL grammars cannot even correspond to any
potential human knowledge. Hence Chomsky's (1981b: 5) radical
conceptualist claim: 'Rather, the linguist is studying mentally-
represented rules and the representations they generate.' can only
be a thorough confusion.

More generally, the doctrine that a grammatical theory should
characterize a collection of NL grammars which are just those
which are learnable by human beings (in the ordinary way) is
completely untenable. This would have, inter alia, the intolerable
consequence that the real bounds on human memory must be part
of grammatical theory, an obvious scientific redundancy precluded by Occam's razor, since these bounds must be part of a
distinct psychological or biological theory about human nature.

The conclusion that there are unlearnable finitely specifiable
NL grammars is not at all paradoxical or surprising. It is a consequence of considerations entirely parallel to those which show
that the collection of humanly performable computations is a
(tiny) subset of the collection of all computations, etc. The confusion of the collection of finitely specifiable NL grammars with the
collection of actually learnable grammars is simply another
special case of the basic confusion of NLs and knowledge of NLs
which pervades both standard and radical conceptualism.

The third defining principle of radical conceptualism is that
grammars are real because they are physically represented (or,
even less sensibly, actually physical) and that NLs are unreal (an
'epiphenomenon'), because they are not physical. To the contrary
however, we have seen that neither grammars nor NLs can be
physical and that even most finite NL grammars have never been
physically represented in real humans and never can be. Moreover, even if there is a physically represented innate grammar-
defining system, this not only does nothing to support Chomsky's

repudiation of NLs, but actually renders it even more incoherent. Further, many non-physical entities must be taken to be real, and are so taken, even by Chomsky. Finally, there is no way that real grammars can fail to characterize NLs, so the supposed unreality of NLs also clashes with the claim that grammars are real. Consequently, the third principle of radical conceptualism fares no better than the first two and can also hardly be taken seriously.

Overall then, the radical conceptualist philosophy of Chomsky's recent writings involves at least three principal interrelated ideas: (i) that grammars generate mental representations of sentences; (ii) that grammars are not responsible for characterizing NLs (i.e. that the adequacy of a posited grammar is not challenged when it is shown that it fails to correspond ccrrectly to the partition of well-formed vs. ill-formed sentences) and (iii) that NLs are not real, though grammars are, because they are physically represented. Together or separately these ideas are so confused and so divorced from reality that it is out of the question to take them as providing a rational ontological framework for linguistics. Consequently, they offer no justified basis for excluding transfinite sentences from the domain of linguistic characterization. Their extraordinarily untenable character is an unintended tribute to the importance of the NL/knowledge of NL or NL/representation of NL distinction, whose implicit rejection underlies them. Such untenable positions can provide no defense of traditional generative linguistic assumptions against the NL Vastness Theorem.

Before concluding our remarks on radical conceptualism, we would like to return to Chomsky's reaction to Hintikka's argument that NLs are not recursively enumerable sets. In his reply to Hintikka, Chomsky supposed that the set of NL sentences of finite length might not be recursively enumerable, even though there is a generative grammar represented in the mind. We criticized this response earlier on methodological grounds, implying that it takes major steps toward eliminating the constraints of factual accountability on grammars. This is made evident by specifying the logic of the reaction:

(9)   a.   Assumption: maximal collections of NL sentences are *not* recursively enumerable sets.
      b.   Psychogrammars are constructive, hence generate recursively enumerable sets.
      c.   (9a) does not show that (9b) is false.

Clearly though, if the claim that a grammar specifies a recursively enumerable set is not falsified by showing that the collection of well-formed sentences is not recursively enumerable, the claim is without factual content.

Putting these severe *methodological* objections aside, there are certain *technical* features worth noting in Chomsky's hinted-at account. They are relevant because it might be imagined that they offer a way to deal with the NL Vastness Theorem as well as with arguments analogous to Hintikka's. The passage cited from Chomsky (1980a: 126) clings (though still without argument) to the traditional generative grammar idea that any humanly acquired grammar *must* be generative, that is, constructive. Quite possibly, the underlying fallacious assumption that a grammar is necessarily constructive prevented Chomsky from adopting the natural conclusion that a *valid* Hintikka-type argument would minimally show that NL grammars are simply not (fully) constructive. In any event, since, for Chomsky, a grammar is constructive, the sentences it characterizes by definition form a recursively enumerable set. But even if an argument like Hintikka's were to show that the collection of sentences of some NL is not recursively enumerable, Chomsky's radical conceptualism still permits the conclusion that the acquired grammars of speakers of that NL are constructive representations of recursively enumerable sets. The acquired grammars just fail to characterize exactly the collection of well-formed sentences.

Such a radical conceptualist sketch purports to offer a reasonable account of a person's having knowledge of a non-recursively enumerable set of sentences. However, discussion of knowing a non-recursively enumerable set only makes sense if it is possible to determine what sentences speakers do and do not have knowledge of. In conceptualist terms though, this is to say that there must, contrary to what Chomsky now claims, be an NL: just the collection of known sentences. To account for this knowledge, Chomsky then in effect proposes a system that determines (but does not generate) a collection of NL sentences of finite length. If, to avoid confusion, this system were, contra Chomsky, called a grammar, this grammar would simply be a not fully proof-theoretic specification of some set. Such a system would consist of a generative grammar plus whatever non-decidable principles distinguish those generated sentences that are truly grammatical from those that are not.

One characteristic of the proposal, then, is that it amounts to little more than word play. (9a) turns out not to falsify (9b) only because the constraints on internalized grammars are weakened via a terminological innovation. Where previously grammars had to characterize maximal collections of well-formed sentences, now these collections are putatively to be characterized by a system, not spelled out in detail, which contains a generative grammar plus other non-constructive principles, but which is arbitrarily not called a grammar. Chomsky's appeal to this device is a transparent attempt to protect his a priori notion of grammars as generative against any possible argument of the sort developed by Hintikka. Interestingly though, the proposal still contains one claim strong enough to be falsified. Namely, for Chomsky's remarks to apply at all, the full non-recursively enumerable collection of sentences would have to be regardable as a subset of a recursively enumerable set.

For an absolutely fundamental technical feature of any scheme like that envisaged by Chomsky, no matter how spelled out, is that the well-formed sentences, the ones in principle known to be grammatical, will be *a proper subset* of the recursively enumerable set generated by the constructive grammar. The 'conditions lacking a decision procedure' function only as 'filters' to eliminate some of the countable superset of sentences actually constructed by the grammar. Consequently, sentences of transfinite length are totally undescribable in such terms. Hence such a system could provide no jump in descriptive power to collections of higher cardinality than countably infinite sets, and thus would offer no way at all to characterize a megacollection of sentences. Put differently, Chomsky's assumptions require inter alia that the total collection of well-formed sentences of an NL be included in some larger collection. But if, as shown by the NL Vastness Theorem, these collections are themselves megacollections, there are, under pain of contradiction, no larger collections. Therefore, even if Chomsky's remarks made sense for non-decidable conditions like that suggested by Hintikka and by Chomsky himself,[15] *which they*

---

[15] Chomsky (1980a: 127) takes seriously the possibility that the distribution of *between* versus *among* might depend on the actual (non-decidable) numerical values of certain expressed functions, and thus that on these grounds, English sentences might fail to form a recursively enumerable set in a way parallel to that

do not, no possible variant of any such hinted-at approach offers any way of coping with the NL Vastness Theorem.

This consequence is rephrasable somewhat differently. A basic premiss underlying Chomsky's reaction to Hintikka's argument is that the 'non-decidability' at issue, if real at all, is localized in some quite peripheral, marginal aspect of the linguistic system. It is an appendage on a basically recursively enumerable set specifiable by a Turing machine. But the proof of the NL Vastness Theorem in (16) of chapter 4 shows that the failure of NLs to be recursively enumerable sets, hence proof-theoretically specifiable, indeed, their failure to be sets at all, lies in one of the most central, fundamental productive or 'recursive' features of NLs, coordination. The arguments in section 4.4 show that the same vastness inheres in relative clause constructions, complement clauses, etc. Given this, there is no way to view NLs as characterized by a constructive grammar with some sort of peripheral non-decidable appendage. As argued in section 5.1, there is no way in which a generative grammar can even be a component of a correct NL grammar.

Although there was never the slightest reason to accept anything like the views advanced by Chomsky in reply to Hintikka, the grounds for rejecting his response are enormously strengthened by the recognition that NLs are megacollections. For the NL Vastness Theorem shows that correct NL grammars cannot be of the generative type claimed by Chomsky to be mentally represented; nor can their grammars be generative devices supplemented with some additions. Chomsky's a priori radical conceptualist idea revealed in his response to Hintikka seems to have been in effect that, no matter what the properties of the collection of well-formed sentences, it would always turn out to be possible to maintain the existence of an internalized *constructive* grammar. But, remarks about the constructive M of section 2 aside, there is no known justifiable basis for this conclusion. This is hardly surprising. If the view that NL grammars are constructive is interpreted as a factual claim about linguistic reality, there cannot fail

---

claimed in Hintikka's argument. Although irrelevant, Chomsky's assumptions did not hold for the actual English words, since the forms are intensional. Their distribution depends not on actual numerical values but on the speaker's *assumptions* about values. Even if the value conditions were undecidable, this would show nothing about the collection of well-formed sentences.

to be potential linguistic facts which could falsify it. The NL Vastness Theorem simply shows that some such *potential* linguistic facts are *actual* linguistic facts.

6.5   Conceptualism: summary

There is then apparently no known argument from any justified or justifiable conceptualist assumptions to the claim that transfinite sentences are not elements of the domain of actual linguistic objects. Put differently, there is no known or anticipated argument from conceptualist assumptions which would justify excluding transfinite sentences from the realm of ontologically proper linguistic entities. While we reject any conceptualist interpretation of linguistics, even such an interpretation justifies no limit of the collection of NL sentences to finite entities. Therefore, even the (in our view misguided) doctrine that grammars must account for a conceptual domain provides no grounds undermining the soundness of the NL Vastness Theorem and thus provides no way to save the generative interpretation of NL grammars from the NL Non-constructivity Theorem.

We have formulated the discussion of the relation between conceptualist ontology and the non-mathematical bases of the NL Vastness Theorem in terms of the existence of sentences of infinite size. But it should be clear that parallel considerations show that nothing in any conceptualist ontology justifies rejecting the principle that NLs are e.g. closed under the coordinate compounding of clauses. That is, there are no grounds in ontological commitments which would justify the claim that coordinate compounds with infinitely many conjuncts lie beyond the bounds of proper linguistic characterization.

Consequently, we conclude that not only is the NL Vastness Theorem a mathematically valid proof, its premises, in particular, that NLs are closed under coordinate compounding, yielding transfinitely long sentences, are all true, and hence its conclusion is a genuine truth about NLs. Therefore, the NL Non-constructivity Theorem is also a genuine truth about NLs. There are no ontological escape hatches.

7

The Characterization of
Transfinite Sentences

7.0 Remarks

Chapter 6 argued that there are no known justifications based on
ontological commitments for excluding transfinite sentences from
the domain of NL characterization. The present chapter goes
beyond the claim that no such exclusion has been justified to a
strong version of the 'opposite' conclusion. It indicates why any
exclusion of transfinite sentences from the proper domain of linguistics would actually be quite absurd. In discussing the matter,
we touch upon various issues which arise from the recognition
that transfinite sentences are an integral part of the domain of
linguistic characterization.

7.1 The platonist existence of transfinite sentences

Even those wishing to reject the idea that NL grammars characterize transfinite sentences must grant that such sentences have at
least a platonist existence and thus are not to be confused with
putative objects like square circles, the set of all sets, even primes
not identical to 2, and consistent, complete axiomatizations of
arithmetic, none of which have any existence whatever. Transfinite
sentences are consistently characterized, well-defined objects, that
is, well-defined within the limits of current knowledge of the
properties of NL sentences in general. They are the extensions of
consistent, well-defined intensional conditions.

It is useful to relate the notion of a transfinite sentence to the
notion of an attested sentence. Clearly, no transfinite sentence is

attested; moreover, no transfinite sentence is even attestable. But this does not distinguish transfinite sentences from large finite ones. Thus no linguist can ignore transfinite sentences on the grounds of their unattestability without equally ignoring almost all finite sentences. The arbitrary and unjustified demand that attention be restricted to attestable sentences would artificially limit NLs to a relatively small number of relatively short sentences. Thus there is no reason to exclude transfinite sentences from the realm of proper linguistic objects just because they are types with no (possible) tokens, for this is also a feature of most finite sentences. Recall the quote from Stoll (1963) in section 2.2.

Looked at in this way, transfinite sentences have a platonist existence for exactly the same reason that huge, unperformable finite sentences do. The nature of sentencehood is such that size is irrelevant. An NL sentence is an object, in fact, a set, with such and such properties, and the sets having such properties include those of all cardinalities. From this viewpoint, transfinite sentences exist because they cannot fail to exist, just as sentences with ten to the hundredth power to the hundredth power words cannot fail to exist. There is, therefore, no doubt that transfinite sentences can be studied mathematically like groups, rings, recursive functions, models, etc. Hence, while one can exclude the set of all sets from consideration within linguistics or any other field merely on the grounds that there is no such thing, the parallel claim is impossible for transfinite sentences.

The view that such objects lie beyond the correct borders of linguistics can only then mean that some principles determine that *linguistics in particular*, because of its independently justified goals, principles, limits, etc., properly does not deal with transfinite sentences. That is, the exclusion of transfinite sentences from the realm of linguistics would have to be justifiably based not on their non-existence but on their lack of relevance. Adoption of this position then implicitly suggests that such sentences must be part of the proper domain of some *other* field of inquiry, to which they are relevant. Return again to examples like (2a–d) of chapter 6, which we repeat:

(1) a. Jack$_1$ and his father$_2$ are visiting relatives.
     b. Jack$_1$ and his father$_2$ and his father's father$_3$ are visiting relatives.

    c. $Jack_1$ and his $father_2$ and his father's $father_3$ and ... and his ... $father_k$ are visiting relatives.

    d. $Jack_1$ and his $father_2$ and his father's $father_3$ and ... and his ... $father_{\aleph_0}$ are visiting relatives.

Those who reject the view that (1d) is an English sentence while accepting the standard generative position that all of (1a–c) are well-formed are, in effect, therefore committed to the following claim. While (1a–c) are both mathematically real objects and, further, internal to the domain of linguistic objects, hence to be characterized in linguistics, (1d) is a mathematically real object, yet external to the realm of *linguistic* objects, hence not to be characterized within linguistics. It is this position, call it FINITE, which we will argue is absurd.

7.2   Excluding transfinite sentences from linguistics

Since structures like (1d) are at least mathematically real objects, some domain of inquiry must deal with them. If, however, one excludes them from linguistics, a *proper* account is impossible. The reason is that the principles needed to characterize structures like (1d) fully and adequately at the very least strongly intersect those needed to characterize those like (1a–c), that is, strongly intersect unquestionably linguistic principles. To put the matter more strongly, there is no known linguistic principle relevant for characterizing finite sentences which is not relevant for transfinite ones. It is then inadmissable to exile structures like (1d) to the realm of mathematics, set-theory, etc., with these conceived of as *distinct* from linguistics.[1]

One way to see this is to consider e.g. French analogues of (1a–d):

    (2)   a. $Jacques_1$ et son $père_2$ visitent des parents.

          b. $Jacques_1$ et son $père_2$ et le père de son $père_3$ visitent des parents.

---

[1] From the platonist point of view, the core discipline of linguistics, concerned with characterizing the nature of NLs, is a logico-mathematical discipline.

    c.   Jacques$_1$ et son père$_2$ et le père de son père$_3$ et ... et
        ... père$_k$ visitent des parents.

    d.   Jacques$_1$ et son père$_2$ et le père de son père$_3$ et ... et
        ... père$_{\aleph_0}$ visitent des parents.

Consider what are, by hypothesis, *correct* grammars of French and English, G(F) and G(E). According to FINITE, G(F) characterizes (2a–c) but not (2d) while G(E) characterizes (1a–c) but not (1d). Moreover, the theory of objects of which G(E) and G(F) are special cases is responsible for characterizing no systems which specify infinite structures.

Evidently, G(F) must characterize a collection *not* containing any of (1a–c), while G(E) must characterize a collection *not* containing any of (2a–c). The consequence that the sentences in (1a–c) are not French sentences must follow from the fact that they contain elements which are not French morphemes, elements which violate the principles of French constituent structure, words which do not obey the rules of French phonology, etc. The parallel implications hold for (2a–c) and English. But, once one formulates (non-constructive) principles which determine inter alia that (1a–c) are English but not French, these very principles can distinguish (1d) from (2d) in exactly the way they distinguish (1a–c) from (2a–c).

In spite of this, according to FINITE, (1d) is either not distinguished from (2d) via appeal to the principles relevant for the finite cases, that is, via appeal to G(E), or, if it is, this is done external to linguistics. Obviously, the first alternative makes no sense; but neither does the second. For it means that some field distinct from linguistics must embody inter alia principles which determine that *père* is a well-formed word but that *father* isn't, that *et* is a conjunction, but that *and* isn't, that French requires (3a) and not *(3b), etc.

    (3)   a.   le père de son père
           b.   *son père (le) père

In short, FINITE requires that some field distinct from linguistics involves accounts containing the rules of French and English grammar. Since the choice of English and French as a source for these examples was entirely arbitrary, it follows that FINITE demands that a field distinct from linguistics contain as principles the detailed language-specific grammatical features of every NL.

Next, consider quadruples like:

(4) a. *John, I think they visited and his father$_1$.
   b. *John, I think they visited and his father$_1$ and his father's father$_2$.
   c. *John, I think they visited and his father$_1$ and his father's father$_2$ ... and ... and ... father$_k$.
   d. *John, I think they visited and his father$_1$ and his father's father$_2$ ... and ... and ... father$_{\aleph_0}$.

Structures like (4a, b) are ill-formed as a result of the restriction discovered by Ross (1967) and referred to as the Coordinate Structure Constraint. Knowledge that (4a, b) are ill-formed is provided by direct intuition. However, intuition is not directly relevant for (4c), since, although finite, it is too big to be mentally manipulated. Nonetheless, reasoning indicates that the principle which determines that (4a, b) fall outside of English does likewise for (4c). If the relevant principle is formulated as one which, for example, in the terms of Johnson and Postal (1980), precludes a successor arc from erasing its predecessor inside a coordinate structure, it is easy to see how this principle, if not deliberately complicated, cannot fail to block (4c). But it also cannot then fail to block (4d). The same consequences follow if, instead, one thinks of the Coordinate Structure Constraint in terms of so-called 'trace theory' as precluding a trace inside a coordinate structure but bound by an antecedent outside that structure.[2]

Assume that the Coordinate Structure Constraint is a true principle of grammar valid for all NLs and hence implicit or explicit in any valid grammatical theory. Yet, according to FINITE, the characterization of (4d) is not to be given within linguistics ... which means exactly that it is to be attributed *neither* to English grammar nor to the theory of grammar. It follows that, contrary to Occam's razor, some non-linguistic theory must redundantly

---

[2] Ross's (1967) original formulation of the Coordinate Structure Constraint treated it as a restriction on the operation of transformational rules. This interpretation of course cannot extend to transfinite sentences. But no argument exists justifying Ross's interpretation against currently available (non-constructive) alternatives.

incorporate the Coordinate Structure Constraint. The only alternative would be a claim that, unlike the huge, unperformable, in fact directly unknowable finite structure (4c), (4d) is not ill-formed for the same reason as (4a, b), does not share the properties which make these violate the constraint. But what could possibly justify such a claim? What could justify grouping the directly unknowable (4c) with the knowable (4a, b) and yet not so grouping (4d)? Moreover, since the choice of the Coordinate Structure Constraint for discussion here was arbitrary, FINITE then in general evidently requires some non-linguistic theory to incorporate *every valid linguistic law.*

These examples suffice to reveal the essential reason why FINITE is an intolerable assumption. It simply ignores the fundamental fact:

(5)   The laws/principles governing transfinite sentences are the same as those governing finite sentences.

But, surely, if the identity of the principles governing two putatively different domains does not suffice to show that in fact they are one domain, nothing could. An analogy might be of some relevance. What sense would there be to a view of (human) biology which claimed that this field was concerned only with people whose height was less than some fixed k, with the implicit assumption that an otherwise biological human being would not be such if it were too tall?

7.3   An account of finite sentences is an account of transfinite sentences

The conceptual/theoretical error of FINITE is expressible somewhat differently as follows. Suppose one succeeds in constructing a finite (set of) statement(s) T such that the collection of all *finite* objects satisfying T under some fixed interpretation is exactly all and only the *finite* sentences of English. T is then a finite non-constructive grammar of the finite part of English. Suppose that T entails no size law, that is, a statement of the form 'x satisfies T and the size of x is greater than γ' is consistent, where γ ranges over all positive cardinals, finite or transfinite. Then, as far as we can see, T itself will be, without alteration, a proper characterization of a domain of non-finite sentences. The necessary and sufficient conditions whose satisfaction brings a finite object under the extension of T and hence characterizes it as an element of English likewise determine that transfinite objects satisfy T. FINITE then amounts to two absurd requirements. First, a theory which, *under a unique interpretation of its non-logical vocabulary,* has both finite and non-finite models, is nonetheless only properly to be regarded as an account of the finite models. This is evidently the same absurdity as claiming about Peano's postulates that they are only a theory of integers less than some k, even though, under a consistent interpretation, the postulates characterize all integers, regardless of their size relation to k. Second, FINITE requires that some field distinct from linguistics formulate theories equivalent to T, but whose extensions are limited to transfinite models.

We conclude that if there is a finite non-constructive characterization of the finite sentences of an NL, that system is the proper characterization of transfinite sentences. Moreover, given the argument of chapter 4, the domain of such transfinite sentences is a megacollection. We see no way then in which one can maintain that finite non-constructive characterizations of the finite sentences of an NL could exist without accepting that these also properly characterize transfinite sentences, unless one can show that (5) is false (see below).

Moreover, although we cannot provide a proof at this point, we do not see how a constructive characterization of the finite sentences of an NL could exist without there also being a non-constructive characterization:

(6) Conjecture:
    If T is a constructive grammar (Turing machine), which recursively enumerates the set of finite sentences u of some NL, then there is a finite non-constructive grammar, T′ such that the collection of all and only the finite objects satisfying T′ under some interpretation is u.

If this conjecture is correct,[3] the existence of any correct grammar at all for the finite sentences of an NL would determine that there

---

[3] Of course, (6) is trivially true if T′ is allowed to reference the set generated by a constructive grammar. In such a case, T′ would simply say that x is a sentence of NL_i if and only if x is a member of the set generated by some constructive grammar G. An interesting version of (6) thus must not involve any reference, implicit or explicit, in the definition of 'T′' to a constructive grammar.

is a single correct non-constructive grammar characterizing trans-finite sentences in the same way it characterizes finite sentences. This means that, given a characterization of the finite sentences, there would always be a *cost-free* characterization of the trans-finite sentences. But FINITE amounts to an injunction always forcing rejection of such cost-free characterizations. This shows the absurdity of FINITE, *even if* the conjecture in (6) is false, or even if, contrary to what we have suggested, such cost-free charac-terizations do not exist on some other grounds. For how can one accept an ontological position which, a priori, would preclude linguistics from interpreting an existing account as a character-ization of the maximally broad domain of linguistic objects, even when this interpretation would cost nothing?

The idea we have expressed that non-constructive grammars of the finite sentences of an NL would also be grammars of trans-finite sentences may ultimately be connected to certain profound theorems of model theory within logic. These theorems indicate that a 'theory' T having models of arbitrary finite size has a model of infinite size, and that, within broad limits, if T has a model of infinite cardinality β, it has models of all transfinite cardinalities higher than β; see Stoll (1963: 420–1), Bell and Slomson (1969: 80–6). If, as in Johnson and Postal (1980), one thinks of NL sen-tences as sets, then the finite sentences of NLs provide their non-constructive grammars with models of arbitrary finite size, thus apparently satisfying the antecedent of the first of these theorems. This would yield as a theorem that grammars have infinite models, and thus, via the second theorem, infinite models of all higher cardinalities. In effect, this would mean that the total exten-sion of such a grammar is a megacollection, and thus might seem to indicate, fascinatingly, an entirely different approach to proving the result reached in chapter 4 concerning the megacollection character of NLs.

Unfortunately, these theorems are not immediately directly applicable to non-constructive grammars, for several reasons. Least importantly, the 'theories' they talk about are based on formally defined languages with fixed properties. It must be shown that NL non-constructive grammars can be formulated within the relevant limits. But, much more fundamentally, the theorems only say that 'theories' having models of one size have 'larger' models. Being purely existential, they do not specify that the 'larger' models involve the same kinds of objects as the smaller models. That is, they do not say that the 'theories' have such 'larger' models under the same interpretations of their vocabulary determining the smaller models. Nonetheless, there is a certain clear connection between these results and our suggestion that proper non-constructive grammars of finite NL sentences would ipso facto be grammars of transfinite sentences. Conceivably, using model-theoretical notions and results, it might ultimately be possible to actually prove that this is the case. If so, it would then be provable that a non-constructive grammar of the countable infinity of finite sentences is a grammar of a megacollection of sentences, yielding, in effect, the result of chapter 4 on an entirely different basis. In any event, the relation between NLs as extensions of non-constructive grammars and these and related results in model theory obviously deserve serious study.

7.4   Linguistic versus purely set-theoretical properties

Our discussion of the correctness of treating transfinite sentences internal to linguistics has been based on principle (5). Of course, we have not demonstrated that (5) is true across the entire range of sentential properties, and see no way to do so. Moreover, we believe that the burden of proof falls on one who would reject (5) to exhibit properties distinguishing finite from transfinite sentences. We have merely considered certain sentential properties and indicated how their distribution is not partitioned by the finite/transfinite distinction. A critic of our view could provide some basis for excluding transfinite sentences from linguistics by exhibiting clear linguistic properties of finite sentences which do not hold of transfinite sentences, or conversely. But it is absolutely necessary that the properties in question be *linguistic* properties, those characterizing the differences between sentences and arbitrary objects. For, obviously, the finite/transfinite distinction itself is a property which partitions the objects into disjoint finite/transfinite collections. This is irrelevant since the distinction is a general set-theoretical property definable over all sets, linguistic or not.

   One can consider the matter as follows. Sentences are sets ... one cannot say sets of what without a substantive theory. In the framework of Johnson and Postal (1980), for instance, they can be regarded as sets of nodes, relational signs, coordinates and two primitive relations called Sponsor and Erase. As sets, sentences necessarily have all true set-theoretical properties. One such property, for instance, is that no finite set can be put in one-to-one correspondence with one of its proper subsets, whereas every infinite set permits just such a correspondence. As observed by E. Keenan (personal communication), one cannot construct an isomorphism between a finite sentence and any of its subparts, while this is possible for transfinite sentences. This is, however, exactly the sort of non-linguistic property which follows simply from the set-theoretical nature of sentences. It is non-linguistic in the same sense that it is a non-linguistic property of a sentence with 22 words that it can be divided into two equal disjoint continuous word sequences each of which can be put in one-to-one correspondence with the words of a sentence with a prime number of words. Sentences with 23 or 24 words lack this property. But this cannot be taken to indicate that one or the other type of sentence is thereby justifiably excluded from the domain of proper linguistic characterization. More generally, one does not take such purely set-theoretical properties of sentences to be significant at all. The reason is that the existence of such properties follows merely from the assumption that sentences are sets (of arbitrary size) with no appeal to any properties discovered through *linguistic* investigation.

At issue is the question of whether transfinite and finite sentences form a single unified domain, a question which can be answered positively by showing that they share linguistic properties and negatively by showing that there are linguistic properties they do not share. In these terms, the claim in (5) that there is a unified sentential domain not linguistically partitioned by the finite/transfinite boundary can be clarified by the following supplementary stipulation:

(7)   The only properties systematically distinguishing transfinite from finite *sentences* of a fixed NL are those which in general distinguish transfinite from finite *sets*.

Thus the claim that there is a unified sentential domain is the claim that the transfinite sentences of a fixed NL differ from the finite sentences of that NL in no way *not entailed a priori by the set-theoretical differences between transfinite and finite sets*. Thus, in particular, the fact that all transfinite sentences can be mapped one-to-one onto subparts, while no finite sentence can be, reveals absolutely nothing about NLs or sentences, since it follows a priori from the nature of the distinction between transfinite and finite sets. This inevitable contrast between transfinite and finite sentences thus can offer no possible basis for avoiding a uniform characterization of all sentences regardless of cardinalities.

7.5   Some issues of linear order and transfinite sentences

An unquestioned feature of finite NL sentences is that (some) of their elements are linearly (left-to-right) ordered. Specifically, we share the widespread agreement that finite NL sentences involve at least three distinct linear orderings, involving (i) a syntactic string of words; (ii) a string of (morpho)phonological elements and (iii) a phonetic string. These orderings are *total orderings* in the set-theoretical sense, that is, involve a *partial order* relation R which is *connected*. A partial order over a set S is a relation which is reflexive, antisymmetric and transitive. A relation R over S is connected if and only if for any two elements x, y in S, either xRy or yRx. Thus a total order over a set S organizes all the elements of S into a chain. The left-to-right orderings of *attested* NL sentences are, moreover, well-orderings in the sense of the theory of ordered sets. The total order relation R is such that for each maximal set S over which R is defined there is a unique first element of R in every non-empty subset of S.

Although the linear orderings of NL elements in attested sentences are well-orderings, it is not clear that this is a lawful feature of NL sentences per se. The reason is as follows. A connected, reflexive, transitive and antisymmetric relation R over a set S is necessarily a well-ordering if S is finite. In fact, an even stronger conclusion holds, as indicated in Kuratowski and Mostowski (1976: 202):

(8)   THEOREM: In a finite non-empty subset X of a linearly ordered set A there is a first element and a last element.

Given this theorem, the fact that the linear orderings of attested NL sentences are well-orderings need not be attributed to any *linguistic* law, since it follows from the purely set-theoretical properties of finite sets. At issue is the following question: is the fact that each ordered sequence of elements in attested NL sentences has both a first and last element a consequence of specific axioms of grammatical theory which specifically assure both these consequences, or is it merely a consequence of the theorem in (8)? This question obviously cannot be answered simply by direct consideration of finite sentences, since either alternative has exactly the same consequences for finite sentences. The issue is whether there are transfinite sentences (or, more generally, constituents), with no beginnings, with no ends, etc.

Evidently, a priori, the simplest theory would allow all varieties of linear orderings, corresponding to the distinct logically possible types of totally ordered sets, illustrated by the ordered sets of integers in (9):

(9) a. $0, 1, 2, 3, \ldots$
     b. $\ldots, 3, 2, 1, 0$
     c. $1, 2, 3, \ldots, 0$
     d. $\ldots, -3, -2, -1, 0, 1, 2, 3, \ldots$

(9a) is the sequence of non-negative integers, a totally ordered set with a first element (0) but no last element, based on the partial order less than (or equal to) of arithmetic. (9b) is the inverse totally ordered set, based on the partial order greater than (or equal to) of arithmetic, with no first element but a last element. (9c) is a total order with both a first (1) and a last (0) element, based on the partial order R, defined over the non-negative integers as follows:

(10) $(\forall a)(\forall b)(aRb \leftrightarrow$
       $(a \neq b \rightarrow (a \text{ is positive and } b = 0 \lor (a \text{ is less than } b))))$

Finally, (9d) is a total order over the negative and positive integers based on the partial order less than or equal to of arithmetic. It has neither a first nor a last element. We see no a priori reason to assume that NLs cannot have transfinite constituents corresponding to all of the order types in (9). If so, one can avoid imposing special axioms specifying that each ordered NL constituent has a first and/or a last element. Since this least restricted view is the simplest, it should be adopted unless some other theoretical grounds surface which suggest the need for such laws. We currently know of none and conclude that the fact that the linear orderings of *attested* sentences all involve both first and last elements, and are thus, in particular, well-orderings, is merely a consequence of the theorem in (8) together with the linguistically 'accidental' fact that attested sentences, hence any of their constituents or subparts, are finite.

The foregoing paragraphs illustrate how transfinite sentences can manifest properties that are not manifested by any finite sentence; for example, not having a beginning constituent. Such properties fall under stipulation (7). Nevertheless, the possibility might arise that two NLs, call them L_1 and L_2, are distinguished only by sentences of transfinite length. For example, in L_1, every sentence of transfinite length has a beginning, but this is not true of L_2, even though the subcollection of sentences of finite length of L_1 is identical to the subcollection of sentences of finite length of L_2. Now consider children who are exposed to sentences of one of these NLs. Clearly, the children will receive no evidence that would enable them to determine whether they are hearing instances of L_1 or L_2. We may suppose that they decide that the language is L_2 on the basis of innately specified principles; but in that case, they not only will not learn L_1, they cannot. Moreover, no matter how many sentences they are exposed to, they will never be induced to change their minds. That is to say that L_1 is not only unlearnable, it is not even identifiable in the limit in the sense of Gold (1967). Or, in the terms of our discussion in section 3.3 and section 5.4, L_1 is an NL having no adequate inductive basis.

Informally, examples like (9) illustrate that infinite sequences can be infinite 'at' different loci. Thus, while every infinite sequence is infinite somewhere, (9d) shows that a sequence can be infinite at more than one point. There is no limit on the number of such points and there is a sense in which some infinite sequences are infinite (almost) 'everywhere'. Technically, what is involved is the set-theoretical notion *dense*. A set U is said to be dense (see Kuratowski and Mostowski (1976: 205)) if it is densely ordered by some relation R. This means that for any two elements a, b of U, there is another element c such that aRc and cRb. Clearly, no finite sentence is non-vacuously dense (all singleton sets are vacuously dense). None of the total orderings in (9) is dense; in each, there are only limited 'points' where the sequence becomes infinite. The question arises whether the absence of denseness, called scattering, which is of course inevitably true of all finite non-single-element constituents is to be attributed to all constituents. Can transfinite constituents of NL sentences be dense? That is, are there transfinite NL constituents which are, in this respect, like the real number continuum?

It might seem that the simplest theory will not impose special axioms banning dense orderings, so that only some concrete grounds should lead to the imposition of such axioms. However, the possibility of dense orderings depends on a set-theoretical conception of sentences which is, a priori, at least consistent with this. In particular, in the terms of Johnson and Postal (1980), revised along the lines previously indicated, it is unclear how to interpret non-terminal nodes in such a way that dense orderings would be a possibility. This matter requires considerable further reflection. At present, we need not take any position on the question of whether transfinite constituents of NL sentences can include dense orderings.

We concluded above that there are no laws determining that all the total orderings of NL constituents have either first or last elements and that hence these orderings are not lawfully well-orderings. This might be wrong. We now suggest that *even if it is*, no serious problems ensue for grammatical theory or individual grammars from the claim that NLs include (a megacollection of) transfinite sentences. If one supposes that the linear orderings of NL sentences are lawfully well-orderings, a theory of sentences must provide for such well-orderings. When this property is related directly to transfinite sentences, there will evidently be infinitely many elements to be ordered. The megacollection of sentences will include those involving $\aleph_1$, $\aleph_2$, etc. elements to be ordered. A linguistic theory recognizing transfinite sentences then needs to incorporate an account of how such transfinite sets are ordered.

As E. Keenan (personal communication) rightly observes, the basic set-theoretical theorem that there is some well-ordering of *every* set (see Fraenkel (1966: 84); Eisenberg (1971: 272–4); Kuratowski and Mostowski (1976: 254)) would not suffice. A real theory cannot merely contain such an existential statement; it must actually specify the sentential relation which provides the ordering, showing, in particular, that the theoretical account of sentences is such that the proposed relation is well-defined over objects of the sort which the theory analyzes sentences to be, that the relation interacts properly with laws and rules referring to linguistic linear ordering, etc. The problem is not trivial, since there are cases of large infinite sets where it is not known how to exhibit an actual relation which provides the well-ordering known to exist. Conceivably then, under the assumption that the linear orderings are well-orderings for all sentences, not only finite ones, left-to-right-ordering in NL sentences could serve as the foundation of an argument undermining the claim, represented in (5), that the properties of finite NL sentences project naturally to transfinite sentences.

However, even if there were a problem here, it is not really of the sort which could undermine (5). For the difficulties of providing well-orderings for infinite sets larger than countably infinite is a general feature of sets independent of the particular linguistic properties which make a set a sentence. Moreover, while specifying linear order for transfinite sentences is an issue to be faced, we believe there is a satisfactory general approach via appeal to ordinal numbers.

For concreteness, consider sentences to be pair networks in roughly the sense of Johnson and Postal (1980). Such objects are based on primitive elements called nodes, which include a collection of non-terminal nodes. In Johnson and Postal (1980), these were identified with the positive integers (greater than 4). But, as noted in footnote 3 of chapter 5, this does not suffice for transfinite sentences. The natural first generalization might be to identify non-terminal nodes with any cardinal numbers whatever, positive or negative. This would allow analogues of the beginningless and endless ordered sets in (9). If, however, contrary to our current view, the necessity arose to impose well-orderings on all transfinite sentences, to guarantee that each linearly ordered constituent had a first element, one could replace the earlier stipulation about cardinals with one no less general, taking non-terminal nodes to be drawn from the full megacollection (Eisenberg (1971: 291–2)) of *ordinal* numbers. This move is parallel to standard assumptions in infinitary logic, where the collection of variables is taken as coterminous with the collection of ordinals; see Chang (1968: 36). We could then specify that each of the three types of linear orderings of a fixed constituent S, finite or transfinite, mentioned above can be regarded as a well-ordering of a set of ordinal numbers, this set being a subset of all the ordinal numbers representing all the non-terminal nodes of S. For transfinite S, the sets of ordinals to be well-ordered would be transfinite.

Significantly, one can go beyond the existential fact that a well-ordering of each such set exists by taking advantage of an important set-theoretical principle, presented as Theorem 5 in Kuratowski and Mostowski (1976: 229):

(11)   Every set of ordinals is well-ordered by the relation $\leqslant$.
In other words, in any non-empty set of ordinals there exists a smallest ordinal.

See also Halmos (1960: 79); Fraenkel (1966: 75); Eisenberg (1971: 292–3) and Stoll (1963: 309). Given this principle, plus the identification of non-terminal nodes with ordinal numbers, the linear orderings required for NL sentences could then be reduced to well-orderings under $\leqslant$, a relation which holds for transfinite ordinals exactly as for finite ordinals.

Consequently, even if, contrary to what seems currently justified, it were necessary to assume that every left-to-right ordering of an NL constituent was not only a total order but a well-order, no particular problems need ensue for the description of transfinite sentences.

We have suggested that transfinite sentences might have properties which superficially would in principle differentiate them from any finite sentences, e.g. constituents with either no first element, no last element, densely ordered constituents, etc. We would like to briefly show that certain apparent paradoxes which arise from the interaction of such assumptions with certain well-known properties of attested sentences are actually completely non-problematical.

Consider first the fact that some linguistic features are clearly determined in attested sentences by the properties of an (immediately) next element. For instance, this is the case with the

CHARACTERIZATION OF TRANSFINITE SENTENCES 173

choice between the alternative forms of the English indefinite article *a/an*, which depends on whether the immediately following word begins with a consonant or a vowel. Suppose this article appeared in some transfinite sentence in a densely ordered nominal constituent, where there is then no next element. Would this not indicate that the choice between the two forms could not be determined and thus either that either choice would be ill-formed or else that either choice would be well-formed, both inconsistent with the situation in any attested sentence? The answer is no; neither of these consequences need be accepted. The reason is that the constraint on *a/an* can be thought of as involving an existential quantification over next elements. The relevant rule would say that if an element is the indefinite article, then there is a next element and if that element begins with a vowel the form of the article is *an*, etc. The implication is that while dense orderings themselves *might* be allowed, particular rules of individual languages would be such as to preclude their occurrence in whole classes of cases. In particular, since the shape choice for the English article depends on a next element, no constituent containing this article can be densely ordered.

The suggestion is then that schematically the rule in question is of the form:

(12)   (∀a)(∀c)(Indef Article(a) ∧ Immediate
       Constituent(a, c) → (∃b)(Immediate
       Constituent(b, c) ∧ Next(b, a) ∧ P(a)))

where P(a) is a conditional saying that the final consonant of the morphophonemic form of *a* is null only if the initial element of *b* is not a vowel. One might have thought to formulate the rule simply as:

(13)   (∀a)(Indef Article(a) → P(a))

However, (12) is true of all attested cases and is a stronger projection from these than (13), which (12) entails, although (13) does not entail (12). Consequently, adopting the principle to pick the strongest possible projections consistent with known facts, we pick (12) as the correct rule. If it seems odd or unnecessarily complicated (for finite sentences) that the rule for *a/an* requires the existence of a next immediate constituent, note that this predicts inter alia the fact that, contrasting with *some* etc. the indefinite article can never be last:

(14)   Give me some/that/one/two/*a(n).

Consider now cases of first and last elements. We have claimed that transfinite constituents in general might not have first elements or last elements. But particular constraints in individual NLs often refer to these. For example, under the account of coordination in chapter 4, it is an invariant fact of attested English sentences that, for conjunctive cases, the coordinate particle in the first conjunct must always be null, while that in the last conjunct can never be null.

(15)   *and/ø Marianne and/ø Louise and/ø Fred and/*ø
       Carol

Compare this with the situation with negative disjunction:

(16)   neither/*ø Marianne nor/ø Louise nor/ø Fred nor/*ø
       Carol

In these cases, however, we see no reason to state the rules other than purely conditionally, that is, as saying that if a is the conjunctive coordinate particle of the first conjunct it is null, and that if it is the coordinate particle of the last conjunct, it is not null. The antecedents of these rules are simply not satisfied in coordinations lacking the appropriate end elements, hence the overall conditionals will be (vacuously) true, causing no problems and no clashes with the facts of finite sentences.

But a situation parallel to the indefinite article case can arise with first and last elements. Consider, for example, English genitive nominals, as in (17), under the assumption that these are characterized as such independent of the clitic element which they must, under most conditions, contain.

(17)   a.   my father's dog
       b.   my father's father's dog
       c.   my father's ... father's dog
       d.   my father's father's ... dog

We are interested in the case where (17c) is transfinite and in what the grammar should say about (17d), a structure with a transfinite genitive nominal having no last element. That is, in (17d) the position indicates the pre-*dog* nominal is genitive and thus, in all finite cases, must end in the possessive case morpheme. Our assumption is that this case is like the definite article situation. The rule involves an existential statement, schematically:

(18) $(\forall a)(\text{Genitive}(a) \rightarrow (\exists b)(b = \text{'}s \land \text{Immediate}$
        $\text{Constituent}(b, a) \land \text{Last}(b, a)))$

This simply says that a genitive nominal has a last element, which is the case marker. This is the strongest projection possible from the attested facts and implies the merely conditional claim that if a morpheme is the last element of a genitive nominal, it is the case marker. But (18) can only be satisfied by transfinite genitive nominal structures with last elements and hence excludes from English all endless genitive nominals.

We take these cases to show that the existence of constraints referring to first and last elements induces no paradoxes for the view that NLs involve transfinite constituents without either first, last or both elements. If the constraints in question are existential, they will simply rule out classes of such consitutents. If they are not, they will be vacuously satisfied in transfinite constituents lacking the relevant extremal elements. In neither case do such constraints reveal any conflict with the view that well-orderings are not axiomatically imposed on all (transfinite) constituents. At the most, they indicate that, in addition to the imposition of well-orderings on all finite constituents via the theorem in (8), well-orderings may also be imposed on certain transfinite constituents because of the existence of certain (existential) grammatical rules in particular NLs. A parallel remark holds for dense orderings.

The major point made in this section is that the inherent set-theoretical differences between transfinite and finite sets imply the possibility of certain contrasts between transfinite and finite sentences. These contrasts are, however, not inconsistent with principle (5), since they fall under stipulation (7). In particular, we have illustrated how transfinite sentences might have novel (from the standpoint of attested sentences) linear ordering properties, with beginningless, endless and both beginningless and endless constituents, without this raising any genuine difficulties for the claim that finite and transfinite sentences form a single unified linguistic realm. Consequently, nothing in this domain offers any grounds supporting the idea that transfinite sentences are external to NLs.

References

Bach, E. (1964) *An Introduction to Transformational Grammars*, Holt, Rinehart and Winston, New York.

(1971) 'Syntax Since *Aspects*', in R. O'Brien (ed.) *Report of the Twenty-Second Annual Round Table Meeting*, Georgetown University Press, Washington, DC.

(1974) 'Explanatory Inadequacy', in D. Cohen (ed.) *Explaining Linguistic Phenomena*, John Wiley & Sons, New York.

Bartsch, R. and T. Vennemann (1972) *Semantic Structures*, Athenäum Verlag, Frankfurt.

Barwise, J. (1968) *The Syntax and Semantics of Infinitary Logic*, Lecture Notes in Mathematics 72, Springer-Verlag, Berlin.

Bell, J. and A. Slomson (1969) *Models and Ultraproducts: An Introduction,* North-Holland Publishing Company, Amsterdam.

Bennett, J. (1976) *Linguistic Behaviour*, Cambridge University Press, Cambridge.

Beth, E. (1959) *The Foundations of Mathematics*, North-Holland Publishing Company, Amsterdam.

Bever, T. (1982) 'Some Implications of the Nonspecific Bases of Language', in L. Gleitman and E. Wanner (eds.) *Language Acquisition: The State of the Art*, Cambridge University Press, Cambridge.

Boolos, G. S. and R. C. Jeffrey (1974) *Computability and Logic*, Cambridge University Press, Cambridge.

Brame, M. (1979) *Essays Toward Realistic Syntax*, Noit Amrofer, Seattle, Washington.

Bresnan, J. (1980) 'The Passive in Lexical Theory', *Occasional Paper #7*, The Center for Cognitive Science, Massachusetts Institute of Technology, Cambridge, Massachusetts.

(1982) *The Mental Representation of Grammatical Relations*, The MIT Press, Cambridge, Massachusetts.

Cantor, G. (1952) *Contributions to the Founding of the Theory of Transfinite Numbers*, Dover Publications Inc., New York.

(1967) 'Letter to Dedekind', in J. van Heijenoort (ed.) *From Frege to Gödel: A Source Book in Mathematical Logic, 1879–1931*, Harvard University Press, Cambridge, Massachusetts.

Chafe, W. (1970a) *A Semantically Based Sketch of Onondaga*, Indiana University Publications in Anthropology and Linguistics, Volume 36, Number 2, Part II, Bloomington, Indiana.

(1970b) *Meaning and the Structure of Language*, The University of Chicago Press, Chicago, Illinois.

Chang, C. (1968) 'Some Remarks on the Model Theory of Infinitary Languages', in J. Barwise (ed.) *The Syntax and Semantics of Infinitary Languages*, Springer-Verlag, Berlin.

Chomsky, N. (1955) *The Logical Structure of Linguistic Theory*, unpublished manuscript, Cambridge, Massachusetts.

(1956) 'Three Models for the Description of Language', *IRE Transactions on Information Theory*, Volume IT-2: 113–24.

(1957) *Syntactic Structures*, Mouton and Company, The Hague.

(1959) 'On Certain Formal Properties of Grammars', *Information and Control* 2: 137–67.

(1963) 'Formal Properties of Grammars', in D. Luce, R. Bush and E. Galanter (eds.) *Handbook of Mathematical Psychology*, Volume II, John Wiley & Sons, New York.

(1965) *Aspects of the Theory of Syntax*, The MIT Press, Cambridge, Massachusetts.

(1972a) *Language and Mind*, Harcourt Brace Jovanovich Inc., New York.

(1972b) 'Some Empirical Issues in the Theory of Transformational Grammar', in S. Peters (ed.) *Goals of Linguistic Theory*, Prentice-Hall Inc., Englewood Cliffs, New Jersey.

(1975) *The Logical Structure of Linguistic Theory*, Plenum Press, New York.

(1977a) *Reflections on Language*, Pantheon Books, New York.

(1977b) *Essays on Form and Interpretation*, North-Holland Publishing Company, Amsterdam.

(1979) *Language and Responsibility*, Pantheon Books, New York.

(1980a) *Rules and Representations*, Columbia University Press, New York/Basil Blackwell, Oxford.

(1980b) Response to comments, *The Behavioral and Brain Sciences* 3.43–4.

(1981a) *Lectures on Government and Binding*, Foris Publications, Dordrecht.

(1981b) 'On the Representation of Form and Function', *The Linguistic Review* 1: 3–40.

(1981c) 'Published Remarks', *Philosophical Transactions of the Royal Society of London* 295: 277–81.

(1982) *Some Concepts and Consequences of the Theory of Government and Binding*, The MIT Press, Cambridge, Massachusetts.

and M. Halle (1968) *The Sound Pattern of English*, Harper & Row, New York.

and H. Lasnik (1977) 'Filters and Control', *Linguistic Inquiry* 8.425–504.

and G. Miller (1963) 'Introduction to the Formal Analysis of Natural Languages', in D. Luce, R. Bush and E. Galanter (eds.) *Handbook of Mathematical Psychology*, Volume II, John Wiley & Sons, New York.

Cummins, R. and R. Harnish (1980) 'The Language Faculty and the Interpretation of Linguistics', *The Behavioral and Brain Sciences* 3: 18–19.

Dedekind, R. (1901) *Essays on the Theory of Numbers*, The Open Court Publishing Company, La Salle, Illinois.

Dik, S. (1968) *Coordination*, North-Holland Publishing Company, Amsterdam.

(1978) *Functional Grammar*, North-Holland Publishing Company, Amsterdam.

(1980) *Studies in Functional Grammar*, Academic Press, New York.

Dowty, D. (1978) 'Governed Transformations as Lexical Rules in a Montague Grammar', *Linguistic Inquiry* 9: 393–426.

(1982) 'Grammatical Relations and Montague Grammar', in P. Jacobson and G. Pullum (eds.) *The Nature of Syntactic Representation*, Reidel and Company, Dordrecht.

Drake, S. (1974) *Set Theory: An Introduction to Large Cardinals*, North-Holland Publishing Company, Amsterdam.

Eisenberg, M. (1971) *Axiomatic Theory of Sets and Classes*, Holt, Rinehart and Winston, New York.

Enderton, H. (1974) *A Mathematical Introduction to Logic*, Academic Press, New York.

Fraenkel, A. (1966) *Set Theory and Logic*, Addison-Wesley Publishing Company, Reading, Massachusetts.

Y. Bar-Hillel and A. Levy (1973) *Foundations of Set Theory*, North-Holland Publishing Company, Amsterdam.

Frege, G. (1977) 'Compound Thoughts', in P. Geach (ed.) *Logical Investigations*, Basil Blackwell, Oxford.

Gazdar, G. (1981a) 'Unbounded Dependencies and Coordinate Structure', *Linguistic Inquiry* 12: 155–84.

(1981b) 'Published Remarks', *Philosophical Transactions of the Royal Society of London* 295: 281–3.

(1982) 'Phrase Structure Grammar', in P. Jacobson and G. Pullum (eds.) *The Nature of Syntactic Representation*, Reidel and Company, Dordrecht.

and G. Pullum (1981) 'Subcategorization, Constituent Order, and the Notion "Head" ', in M. Moortgat, H. van der Hulst and T. Hoekstra (eds.) *The Scope of Lexical Rules*, Foris Publications, Dordrecht.

Gödel, K. (1964) 'What is Cantor's Continuum Problem?', in P. Benacerraf and H. Putnam (eds.) *Philosophy of Mathematics*, Prentice-Hall Inc., Englewood Cliffs, New Jersey.

Gold, E. (1967) 'Language Identification in the Limit', *Information and Control* 10: 447–74.

Greenberg, J. (1957) *Essays in Linguistics*, Viking Fund Publications in Anthropology Number 24, Wenner-Gren Foundation, New York.

Gross, M. (1972) *Mathematical Models in Linguistics*, Prentice-Hall Inc., Englewood Cliffs, New Jersey.

Halmos, P. (1960) *Naive Set Theory*, D. Van Nostrand Company Inc., Princeton, New Jersey.

Hardy, G. H. (1941) *A Mathematician's Apology*, Cambridge University Press, Cambridge.

Harmon, G. (1963) 'Generative Grammars Without Transformational Rules: A Defense of Phrase Structure', *Language* 39: 597–616.

Harris, Z. (1968) *Mathematical Structures of Language*, Interscience Publishers, John Wiley & Sons, New York.

Hays, D. (1964) 'Dependency Theory: A Formalism and Some Observations', *Language* 40: 511–25.

Hilbert, D. (1967) 'On the Foundations of Logic and Arithmetic' in J. van Heijenoort (ed.) *From Frege to Gödel: A Source Book in Mathematical Logic, 1879–1931*, Harvard University Press, Cambridge, Massachusetts.

Hintikka, J. (1977) 'Quantifiers in Natural Languages: Some Logical Problems 2', *Linguistics and Philosophy* 1: 153–72.

Hockett, C. (1966) *Language, Mathematics and Linguistics*, Mouton and Company, The Hague.

(1968) *The State of the Art*, Mouton and Company, The Hague.

Hopcroft, J. and J. Ullman (1979) *Introduction to Automata Theory, Languages, and Computation*, Addison-Wesley Publishing Company, Reading, Massachusetts.

Hudson, R. (1971) *English Complex Sentences*, North-Holland Publishing Company, Amsterdam.

(1976) *Arguments for a Non-transformational Grammar*, The University of Chicago Press, Chicago, Illinois.

Johnson, D. (1979) *Toward a Theory of Relationally-Based Grammar*, Garland Publishing Inc., New York.

   and P. Postal (1980) *Arc Pair Grammar*, Princeton University Press, Princeton, New Jersey.

Joshi, A., S. Kosaraju and H. Yamada (1972) 'String Adjunct Grammars: I', *Information and Control* 21: 93–116.

Kac, M. (1980) 'Corepresentational Grammar', in E. Moravcsik and J. Wirth (eds.) *Syntax and Semantics, Volume 13: Current Approaches to Syntax*, Academic Press, New York.

Karp, C. (1964) *Languages with Expressions of Infinite Length*, North-Holland Publishing Company, Amsterdam.

Katz, J. (1966) *The Philosophy of Language*, Harper & Row, New York.

   (1972) *Semantic Theory*, Harper & Row, New York.

   (1977) 'The Real Status of Semantic Representations', *Linguistic Inquiry* 8: 559–84.

   (1978) 'Effability and Translation', in F. Guethner and M. Guethner-Reuter (eds.) *Meaning and Translation: Philosophical and Linguistic Approaches*, New York University Press, New York.

   (1980) 'Chomsky on Meaning', *Language* 56: 1–41.

   (1981) *Language and Other Abstract Objects*, Rowman and Littlefield, Totowa, New Jersey/Basil Blackwell, Oxford.

   (1983) 'An Outline of Platonist Grammar', in T. Bever, J. Carroll and L. Miller (eds.) *Talking Minds: The Study of Language in Cognitive Science,* The MIT Press, Cambridge, Massachusetts.

Keenan, E. (1980a) 'Passive is Phrasal (Not Sentential or Lexical)' in T. Hoekstra, H. van der Hulst and M. Moortgat (eds.) *Lexical Grammar,* Foris Publications, Dordrecht.

   (1980b) 'A Conception of Core Grammar', unpublished manuscript.

Keisler, H. (1971) *Model Theory for Infinitary Logic*, North-Holland Publishing Company, Amsterdam.

Kleene, S. (1952) *Introduction to Metamathematics*, D. Van Nostrand Company, Princeton, New Jersey.

Koster, J. (1981) 'Configuration Grammar', in R. May and J. Koster (eds.) *Levels of Syntactic Representation*, Foris Publications, Dordrecht.

Kreisel, G. (1964) 'Hilbert's Programme', in P. Benacerraf and H. Putnam (eds.) *Philosophy of Mathematics*, Prentice-Hall Inc., Englewood Cliffs, New Jersey.

Kuratowski, K. and A. Mostowski (1976) *Set Theory*, North-Holland Publishing Company, Amsterdam.

Lakoff, G. and H. Thompson (1975) 'Introducing Cognitive Grammar', in C. Cogen et al. (eds.) *Proceedings of the First Annual Meeting of the Berkeley Linguistic Society*, Berkeley Linguistics Society, Berkeley, California.

Lakoff, R. (1971) 'If's, And's and But's About Conjunction', in C. Fillmore and T. Langendoen (eds.) *Studies in Linguistic Semantics*, Holt, Rinehart and Winston, New York.

Lamb, S. (1966) *Outline of Stratificational Grammar*, Georgetown University Press, Washington, DC.

Lambek, J. (1961) 'On the Calculus of Syntactic Types', in R. Jakobson (ed.) *Structure of Language and Its Mathematical Aspects*, American Mathematical Society, Providence, Rhode Island.

Langendoen, T. (1964) 'Formal Linguistic Theory and the Theory of Abstract Automata: An Informal Discussion', unpublished paper.

(1976) 'On the Weak Generative Capacity of Infinite Grammars', *CUNY Forum* 1: 13–24.

(1978) 'On the Assignment of Constituent Structures to the Sentences Generated by a Transformational Grammar', *CUNY Forum* 8: 1–32.

(1982) 'The Grammatical Analysis of Texts', in S. Allén (ed.) *Text Processing: Proceedings of Nobel Symposium 51*, Almqvist and Wiksell, Stockholm.

Lapointe, S. (1977) 'On Guaranteeing the Recursiveness of Natural Languages', in A. Ford, J. Reighard and R. Singh (eds.) *Papers from the Sixth Meeting of the North Eastern Linguistic Society*, Montreal Working Papers in Linguistics, Volume 6, Université de Montréal, Montreal.

Lees, R. (1960a) *The Grammar of English Nominalizations*, Indiana University Research Center in Anthropology, Folklore and Linguistics, Bloomington, Indiana.

(1960b) 'What are Transformations?', in J. McCawley (ed.) *Syntax and Semantics 7: Notes from the Linguistic Underground*, Academic Press, New York.

(1965) 'On the Testability of Linguistic Predicates', *Linguistics* 12: 37–48.

Lewis, H. and C. Papadimitriou (1981) *Elements of the Theory of Computation*, Prentice-Hall Inc., Englewood Cliffs, New Jersey.

Lockwood, D. (1972) *Introduction to Stratificational Linguistics*, Harcourt Brace Jovanovich Inc., New York.

Longacre, R. (1964) *Grammar Discovery Procedures*, Mouton and Company, The Hague.

Mel'čuk, I. (1981) 'Meaning-Text Models: A Recent Trend in Soviet Linguistics', *Annual Review of Anthropology: 1981* 10: 27–62.

Miller, G. and N. Chomsky (1963) 'Finitary Models of Language Users', in D. Luce, R. Bush and E. Galanter (eds.) *Handbook of Mathematical Psychology*, Volume II, John Wiley & Sons, New York.

Neumann, J. von (1925) 'Eine Axiomatisierung der Mengenlehre', *Mathematische Zeitschrift* 27: 669–752.

Neumann, J. von (1967) 'An Axiomatization of Set Theory' in J. van Heijenoort (ed.) *From Frege to Gödel: A Source Book in Mathematical Logic, 1879–1931*, Harvard University Press, Cambridge, Massachusetts.

Okabe, H. (1980) 'Formal Expression of Infinite Graphs and Their Families', *Information and Control* 44: 164–86.

Osherson, D. and S. Weinstein (1982) 'A Note on Formal Learning Theory', *Cognition* 11: 77–88.

Partee, B. (1975) 'Montague Grammar and Transformational Grammar', *Linguistic Inquiry* 6: 203–300.

(1976) *Montague Grammar*, Academic Press, New York.

Peters, S. and R. Ritchie (1973) 'On the Generative Power of Transformational Grammars', *Information Sciences* 6: 49–83.

Postal, P. (1964) 'Underlying and Superficial Linguistic Structure', *Harvard Educational Review* 34: 246–66.

(1966) Review of R. Dixon, *Linguistic Science and Logic, Language* 42: 84–93.

(1970) 'Linguistic Anarchy Notes' in J. McCawley (ed.) *Syntax and Semantics 7: Notes from the Linguistic Underground*, Academic Press, New York.

(1982) 'Some Arc Pair Grammar Descriptions', in P. Jacobson and G. Pullum (eds.) *The Nature of Syntactic Representation*, Reidel and Company, Dordrecht.

Pullum, G. (1982) 'Free Word Order and Phrase-Structure Rules', in J. Pustejovsky and P. Sells (eds.) *Proceedings of NELS 12*, Graduate Linguistics Student Association, University of Massachusetts, Amherst, Massachusetts.

(1983) 'How Many Possible Human Languages Are There?', *Linguistic Inquiry* 14: 447–67.

and G. Gazdar (1982) 'Natural Languages and Context-Free Languages', *Linguistics and Philosophy* 4: 471–504.

Putnam, H. (1975a) *Mathematics, Matter and Method: Philosophical Papers Volume 1*, Cambridge University Press, Cambridge.

(1975b) *Mind, Language and Reality: Philosophical Papers Volume 2*, Cambridge University Press, Cambridge.

Quine, W. (1953) *From a Logical Point of View*, Harvard University Press, Cambridge, Massachusetts.

(1963) *Set Theory and Its Logic*, Harvard University Press, Cambridge, Massachusetts.

Reich, P. (1969) 'The Finiteness of Natural Language', *Language* 45: 831–43.

Rosenbloom, P. (1950) *The Elements of Mathematical Logic*, Dover Publications, New York.

Ross, J. (1967) *Constraints on Variables in Syntax*, MIT Doctoral Dissertation, Cambridge, Massachusetts.

Russell, B. (1903) *The Principles of Mathematics*, Norton and Company, New York.

Sanders, G. (1972) *Equational Grammar*, Mouton and Company, The Hague.

Schachter, P. (1978) Review of R. Hudson, *Arguments for a Non-transformational Grammar, Language* 54: 348–76.

Scott, D. (1965) 'Logic with Denumerably Long Formulas and Finite Strings of Quantifiers', in J. W. Addison, L. Henkin and A. Tarski (eds.) *The Theory of Models*, North-Holland Publishing Company, Amsterdam.

(1973) 'Background to Formalization' in H. Leblanc (ed.) *Truth, Syntax and Modality*, North-Holland Publishing Company, Amsterdam.

Slezak, P. (1982) 'Gödel's Theorem and the Mind', *British Journal for the Philosophy of Science* 33: 41–52.

Stoll, R. (1963) *Set Theory and Logic*, W. H. Freeman and Company, San Francisco.

Wall, R. (1972) *Introduction to Mathematical Linguistics*, Prentice-Hall Inc., Englewood Cliffs, New Jersey.

Wexler, K. (1982) 'On Extensional Learnability', *Cognition* 11: 89–96.

P. Culicover and H. Hamburger (1975) 'Learning-Theoretic Foundations of Linguistic Universals', *Theoretical Linguistics* 2: 215–53.

and P. Culicover (1980) *Formal Principles of Language Acquisition*, The MIT Press, Cambridge, Massachusetts.

Woods, W. (1970) 'Transition Network Grammars for Natural Language Analysis', *Communications of the ACM* 13: 10–38.

Zadeh, L. (1965) 'Fuzzy Sets', *Information and Control* 8: 338–53.

Ziff, P. (1974) 'The Number of English Sentences', *Foundations of Language* 11: 519–32.

Index